Clár áb[...]
Table of Contents

Cuid a Dó – Part Two

Ag Cothú na Tine – Fuelling the Fire

Réamhrá
Introduction

What if a language you thought was lost, buried or too daunting was there waiting for you all along, ready to spark something powerful within you? Well, I'm here to guide you on a journey that will enable you to take ownership of **an Ghaeilge** – the Irish language – and allow you to immerse yourself in its beauty, its culture and customs, and its history, which are all **fite fuaite** – interwoven – in its relationship with Hiberno-English. Maybe it's about rekindling the embers for you, or striking the first match. Either way, set the glow alight and soon you will be shining brightly! The path is illuminated for you.

I will show you how simple and useful Irish can be in your life, and clarify concepts that once seemed so dense. Together, we will explore the meaning in our daily phrases and the psyche of our interactions. This guide will make you rethink and revitalise **ár dteanga** – our language. Spark your connection with Irish: start where you are, use what you have, and be part of this global process of keeping our indigenous language alive. Language is culture. Discover the hidden gems, the practical nuggets, the intricate systems that make up this unique and lyrical, hilarious and beautiful mother tongue.

The Irish language is full of **seanfhocail** – wise sayings or proverbs – and I have thought of my own personal favourite that captures the essence of the learning journey, which begins with lighting the spark of intention: **cuir lasóg ar an tine** – put a little light to the fire.

A language can lie dormant, a tiny glow in the embers waiting for a breath of air and some fresh kindling to revive the flame. The sparks of my own journey came intergenerationally, a flame carried by my grandmother. An Irish speaker, Mary Guidera was one of the most influential people in my life growing up and her words of encouragement were fuel to my fire. **Grá mór** – big love, she would say whenever we spoke. She encouraged me in every challenge, celebrated every triumph, and bestowed at all times, without condition, her grandmotherly love. She set alight my passion for our language.

Fanning that flame has illuminated my understanding of our culture, identity and heritage, and inspired me to help others in the same pursuit. It has shed light on the richness and alignment we can bring into our lives. So, how do we best nourish the fire – **beathú a chur ar an tine?** How do we let a curiosity catch, and set it ablaze? I've written this book to help light the way on your Irish language journey, a route to belonging, to connection with the past, to greater freedom within. Together we can turn a spark into a blaze. Fire is, after all, the only element that can make more of itself.

To start, let me tell you a little more about my own torch-carrying path. Like all good journeys, its destination was not clear at the outset …

Cuid a hAon
Part One

....

Cuir Lasóg ar an Tine
Ignite the Fire

1

Ó Splanc go Lasair: Mo Thuras Gaeilge
From Spark to Flame: My Gaeilge Journey

I didn't grow up in the Gaeltacht or an Irish-speaking household. Irish is not my first language. Yet somewhere along the way, a tiny spark for my native language began to flicker – one I didn't fully recognise or acknowledge at the time, but one that would grow to become an integral part of my life.

The first time I remember having a tangible feeling about the Irish language was the sense of pride I felt when my American cousins came over to spend Thanksgiving with us in Dublin. I was seven years old, and I took on the role of Chief Culture Officer, showing my cousin's new wife my Irish dancing steps, and creating a little booklet for her with the numbers and colours in Irish.

At school, despite it not being a **Gaelscoil** – Irish-medium school – the daily instructions were all in Irish. Frequent orders included **cuirigí bhur gcathaoireacha ar an mbord** – put your chairs on the table – and **tógaigí amach bhur mboscaí lóin** – take out your lunch boxes. The teachers would have hurried whispers of private conversations in Irish so we wouldn't understand. At home, my family were positive about Irish, my mum being a primary school teacher, and my Nana attending Irish evening classes and a **ciorcal comhrá** – conversation circle.

There are old home videos of me performing poems half in Irish and half in English, having written them to celebrate a birthday or my grandparents' wedding anniversary. It shows a time when playing with the language was normalised, when I spoke confidently and laughed at my mispronunciations and danced between the two languages with a child's carefree nonchalance.

Secondary school quickly extinguished the flame and warped the language into an academic subject, burdened with pressure and devoid of fun. To go down the traditional route, in order to get an A in Irish in the Leaving Certificate (the final state exams), we students found ourselves memorising a script, regurgitating answers, and attending expensive, intensive grinds. It is typical to find ambitious students who can write essays on various social problems, but cannot have a conversation. Nor do they connect the language with ancestry, culture or identity. With very little opportunity or practice producing the language, apart from in contrived, learned-off expressions and structures, there is no spontaneity or natural communication. I once cheekily asked our Irish teacher what led him to teaching. He instantly quipped, 'June, July and August, girls.' That is, three months off each summer. The mad thing is, I don't remember him ever speaking any Irish. **Nach bhfuil sé sin craiceáilte?** – Isn't that crazy?

My Spanish teacher, on the other hand, would lead us in a Hail Mary in Spanish at the beginning of every lesson, and I can recall that prayer on command. She lived the language. She was intentional, passionate, proud and persuasive. She would organise Spanish breakfasts once per term, where she'd bake a *tortilla* and we would enjoy *desayuno* – breakfast – as a group. That is what makes the difference. Six years of learning Spanish versus fourteen years learning Irish and I felt ready to immerse myself in Spanish, but uncomfortable using Irish. I felt reasonably confident with Spanish and, if not confident, at least not traumatised. I could hold a conversation. I didn't worry about making mistakes. I could talk around a subject if I didn't know the exact words to get a point across. The teacher was available and engaging. When we feel positive and supported, we thrive. **Creid é nó ná creid** – believe it or not, the difference between a student who *believes* they can learn, and one who doesn't believe it at all, is everything.

Ironically, the motto of the Gaeltacht I was kicked out of when I was thirteen years old was **'Is fiú agus is féidir'** – It's worth it and you can do it. I was sent home on the train from **Gaillimh** – Galway – to **Baile Átha Cliath** – Dublin – crying my eyes out, after saying eight words **as Béarla** – in English. I wish I could say it was down to the practice of traditional Irish teaching methods at the time, but even contemporary education can be punitive and counter-intuitive, and is perpetuated by the false narratives around language learning and the misconceived core beliefs we have about our own native language.

That initial bad experience did not deter me, however, and I returned the following year and in subsequent years. Three weeks in remote Conamara, sleeping fourteen to a room, staying up way past lights out, trying to catch the make-up thief and being woken up with a **'Seachain do chuid Béarla!'** – Watch your English! – did have a profound effect on my Irish fluency and my respect for the language. I became a **cinnire** – prefect, and then **príomhchinnire** – head girl.

Back at school, the language being treated as just a school subject dulled the spark of love for the language that the Gaeltacht had ignited in me. I did as I was told, and got an A in the Leaving Cert. After graduating, apart from the rare token expression, Irish fell off my radar. I loved reading and writing, so I chose to study English at Trinity College, Dublin and spent four wonderful years there. During the summers, I travelled around India, built a house in South Africa as a volunteer with Habitat for Humanity and had a brief stint in Ibiza with an organisation that helped party-goers in the San Antonio nightclubs get home safely (or get to a hospital safely) but **sin scéal eile** – that's another story!

When I graduated, I had my sights set on the world of publishing or communications, but life threw an opportunity at me, and I thought, 'take more chances, dance more dances'! A friend called to say her employer at a summer camp in the Swiss Alps was hiring an equestrian to be 'pony girl' and asked would I like a job? Yes, I would! Next thing I know I'm on a funicular up a steep ravine. I invested what I earned that first summer in a Cambridge

Celta course – Certificate of English Language Teaching for Adults, a teaching qualification that taught me, I attest, how to teach anything!

This qualification opened doors for me in top international language academies, and I got my first job teaching English in a small town in the heart of the Basque Country in northern Spain. While the classroom was rewarding, there was a hum of conflicted feelings nudging me about the fact that my students needed English to advance in their education, to access university, to move abroad and heighten career prospects, but that it was detrimental to the value put on their ancient language. Thankfully, in that part of the Basque Country, the Euskera language is spoken daily **sa phobal** – in the community. It was inspiring, uplifting and mesmerising. To live in the Basque Country and speak Spanish – but not Basque – was a life half-lived. To speak with local people in their own language, even making a small effort, affords you insights to the culture and history that a monolingual speaker will never enjoy.

It was there that I began to reflect on the language I had left behind. The one many of us tend to leave behind. It's where I not only understood, but felt keenly my privilege of being a native English speaker. It awakened a consciousness in me of my relationship with the English language and with my own indigenous language, with my accent and my special version of English. A habitable grief. As Blue Niall, the rapper, producer and artist, put it in a podcast episode with me – 'our two imperfect modes of expression'. We add poetry and flavour to English, a language we communicate with but which doesn't hold cultural currency, and can feel lost at sea in our own ancestral tongue.

Despite the idyllic situation in the Basque village, I knew the world was enticing me onwards and upwards, towards more adventure, so I left the school and moved to Budapest and then Córdoba. I did voice-overs and accent coaching and specialised in early childhood teaching and exam preparation. The more time I spent away from Ireland, the greater the sense of **cumha** – homesickness, grief, longing, and a **cumhacht** – power. An expansiveness afforded to me by being away from Ireland, and missing it, was lingering.

My Nana was by that time living in a nursing home in Dublin and I would call her regularly. She was becoming very deaf and it was difficult to have a phone conversation, but when I switched to Irish one day, we had the most glorious chat. Every phone call, every birthday card, every conversation with her would finish with **grá mór** – big love. She ignited in me this **grá** for **Gaeilge**, and while I sometimes wish I had spoken more Irish to her when I had the chance, I have to practice what I teach – **ná coinnigh do bhrón mar bhrón** – don't keep your sadness as sadness. Turn it into goals.

Living life without regrets led me to my next job teaching English and Zumba on the Peace Boat, a UN-accredited NGO that sets sail from Japan and navigates around the world stopping at 30 or 40 ports over four or five months, and invites academics and activists to give lectures on human development, rights, peace studies and conflict resolution. I met guests like Ela Gandhi (Mahatma Gandhi's granddaughter) and José Mujica (the former president of Uruguay). I organised the St. Patrick's Day festivities on board, and very soon had a daily top-deck Irish dancing club who were happy with my sparse knowledge of The Walls of Limerick, and wanted to perfect the dance. Meanwhile, an international online language platform I had worked for saw that I had Irish listed as one of my languages. They aim to offer every language in the world, and so they encouraged me to offer Irish tuition.

Yes, I was ready: ready to not be ready, but to say yes anyway. The exploration of English, breaking it down, putting it back together, interrogating its structures and sounds, had prepared me, and I knew I would be able to apply those teaching skills to our own **Gaeilge**.

My first student was a woman in Florida who wanted to propose to her girlfriend in Irish. Soon I had students from all over the world. I received requests from druids and Celtic priestesses, families who wanted to move to Ireland, genealogists and of course all the Duolingo devotees. Overcome with emotion and appreciation, some of them burst into tears as they started to speak Irish – and enjoy, understand and use what they were learning.

Time zones apart, we were connected, with our notebooks and coffee and bright smiles and earnestness. Designing a curriculum, informed by my research on learning strategies and language teaching methodologies, was thrilling. I was able to reveal the patterns, logic and satisfying structures of the language that were never explained to me in school. I was unravelling and undoing the conditioning. I was discovering such depths of beauty and wisdom in the language, and found fulfilment in sharing it with my students. I read voraciously online, scouring dictionaries and translating grammar books into more accessible, joyful, engaging, user-friendly resources. At that time there was a dearth of materials and what existed was dry and off-putting, but I devoured forums where people would argue over the nitty gritty of the grammar. I enrolled in advanced courses myself to upskill and to boost my accuracy and fluency. I spent time in different Gaeltacht regions to study nuances in the different dialects and to broaden my knowledge. I began to shake myself free from feelings of inadequacy. The phrase 'imposter syndrome' is not a native Irish one, and my Nana had taught me that 'failure is not in your vocabulary'.

I was now self-employed full time, and made the decision to teach Irish only. I realised that teaching Irish was something I looked forward to and found purpose in. It was so meaningful for me to explore the intricacies and indigenous insights that lit up this language.

Go tobann – suddenly my calendar was overflowing and my students were accelerating their learning. I mean, the giddy goats were waking up at 3am for lessons, talking to their horses in Kentucky through Irish, writing wedding speeches in Irish, learning the songs their grandfather sang to them when they were young. They were getting excited to properly understand the **Modh Coinníollach** – Conditional Mood (or tense) – and the **Tuiseal Ginideach** – genitive case – the two bad boys of the grammar books. My students couldn't fathom why kids and teenagers in Ireland gave out about their free, daily, hour-long lessons. While students in Ireland were learning the language mindlessly off by heart, these enthusiasts were learning *from* the heart and with an open mind.

But when I told people in Ireland that I taught Irish, they asked 'Who the hell would want to learn Irish?'

I had to challenge the stigma around our native language. I set up social media accounts – **Irish with Mollie** – and shared short videos teaching words and expressions, etymology and learning resources. My aim was to reach more people and spread the language – to demystify it, to democratise it and to let you know it's *yours*. The videos resonated with people and soon I was being recognised on the street, interviewed by *The Irish Times*, invited to speak at festivals and on the radio and being called a 'language healer'. I created self-paced courses with on-demand materials, and now I have over 9,000 students in over 70 countries, a podcast, a newsletter and immersive retreats. We have conversation groups where we chat away all day, every day, and I have students who are moving to the Gaeltacht to start jobs using their Irish, setting up their own communities around the world and being awarded scholarships.

Since 2022, I've made thousands of hours of video, and in each one I imagine I am speaking to my Nana. When she died, I cried and I cried. It's hard to deal with the reality of someone you love so much not being there anymore. I have early memories of wishing and praying that she would live forever. I arrived at the funeral home the morning of the Mass because I had flown in from abroad, and my family had been there the previous night, so they let me go in and see her on my own. She was beautiful and peaceful. My brother and his girlfriend came in and we stood around her in silence. My brother's girlfriend is a fluent Irish speaker and she asked if I would like her to do the rosary **as Gaeilge.**

Sé do bheatha, a Mhuire, atá lán de ghrásta, tá an Tiarna leat. Hail Mary, full of grace, the Lord is with thee.

Hearing the words fill the room, their rhythmic hum buoying us along, was deeply meditative and calming. It being in Irish was soothing, meaningful and almost ethereal. It gave me a sense of resilience, that life goes on, that she lives in the language, and that the language connects us and allows us to weave around this thread stretching back over time to all our ancestors.

I sometimes have audiences of up to 2,000 workshop participants from all over the world, and a social media following of over 300,000 – but I remember her words and I picture her face. She would say, 'When you're speaking Irish thoughtfully, **cloiseann tú gach uile litir** – you hear every single letter'. Even the silent ones. Those pregnant pauses. That breathy, aspirant 'th', those 'i's and slender endings we smile into. This might come as a shock to you if you see a word like **aghaidh** – face, and I'm trying to convince you that it sounds exactly like it's written. It's true, though. Irish, in its orthographic shallowness, is a highly consistent, patterned and logical language. This 'shallowness' isn't a slight – it means the relationship between the sounds of the spoken language and the letters used to write them down is clear and consistent. Any time you meet a 'th' or a 'gh' or an 'ál', it will act the same way as the language follows a set pattern. It's very satisfying to learn. What my Nana meant was that you hear every valley, every peak, the nuances and inflections – the music and a palpable multi-sensory synaesthesia feeling of it. The rhythms that rise from the landscape.

This journey has taught me about belief. We need to believe in our own power to harness it, believe in a bilingual Ireland in order to create it. My vision is to experience

Ireland as a safe and encouraging space to celebrate and promote our language, where people are excited to keep it alive for future generations, and generate the love that is so abundant in it to preserve our legacy as a humane, friendly, warm and inclusive people and place.

2

Feasacht
Awareness

The Irish language is not complicated. It is our complicated relationship with it that distances us from our tongue. An unlearning needs to take place. We must unravel what we think we know.

There is no verb *to know* in Irish, since knowledge comes and goes, is learned and is corrected over time. We simply say, **tá a fhios agam** – the knowledge of it is at me. No ownership or possession; it comes to me. A lot of students tell me that learning Irish feels more like remembering than learning something new.

To open an awareness, a consciousness, a curiosity, an eagerness, a pride and a passion is a necessary part of the journey.

The key to knowing is disentangling how we were taught or what we thought, and making way for an enlightening. **Maraíonn amhras brionglóidí** – doubt kills dreams, but **maraíonn comhsheasmhacht amhras** – consistency kills doubt.

Consistency kills laziness. One word for 'laziness' in Irish is **falsacht**. This also means 'falsity'. We might not link these two words in English, but Irish accepts and assumes that there is a sense of falsehood to being lazy. It is defined as idleness or the quality of being *unwilling* to work, and it is the unwillingness that stands out here. And speaking of standing, consistency is taking a stand. The word **comhsheasmhacht** for consistency literally means 'co-standing' – conjuring ideas of durability, stability and evenness. Another favourite word of mine is **dianseasmhacht** – strict standing, perseverance.

An excuse is a half story. **Leithscéal** – excuse comes from **leith** (half) and **scéal** (story). To say, *excuse me*, we say **gabh mo leithscéal** – take my half story.

The truth of the language shines. This makes me think of that cheeky knowing smile that you might see Irish people wearing, like there is a hidden depth to what they're saying.

Once a person learns something, they retain it, often without realising. This is particularly true in relation to language. In a 2017 study in *Cognition* by Jiyoun Choi, Anne Cutler, and Mirjam Broersma called 'Preserved Implicit Knowledge of a Forgotten Childhood Language', we see this retreat to early language as a natural part of the aging process. Many of my students have told me how they have bonded with their elderly parents and relatives through Irish, as I did with my own Nana, amazed that a person they loved who might have trouble remembering more recent details and memories about their life, could still speak or sing in Irish. Language is deeply embedded within us.

A great way to foster engagement with anyone, **óg nó sean** – young or old, and to help them feel understood and connected is to listen, regardless of your level of Irish. You can help them and their wellbeing by using some of these phrases:

- **Múin é dom** /MOO-win ay dum/ – Teach it to me
- **Abair é arís** /OBB-er ay ar-eesh/ – Say it again
- **An féidir leat é a rá arís?** /on fay-djer lat ay a raw ar-eesh/ – Can you say it again?
- **Ní thuigim** /nee HIGG-um/ – I don't understand

- **Inis dom** /INN-ish dum/ – Tell me
- **Tá mé ag éisteacht** /taw may egg AYSH-tokkt/ – I am listening

The following poem often comes to mind when I think about the deep connection that comes from truly listening and responding to others, whether in Irish or in another language.

Labhair an teanga Ghaeilge liom
Speak the Irish Language to Me

Ó labhair an teanga Ghaeilge liom
Oh speak the Irish language to me
A chuid mo chroí is a stór
My treasure and my darling
An teanga a labhair mo mháthair liom
The language which my mother spoke to me
In Éirinn ghlas fadó
In green Ireland long ago

'Sí teanga bhinn ár sinsear í
It's the sweet language of our ancestors
An chaint is milse ghlór
The sweetest sounding speech
Ó labhair an teanga Ghaeilge liom

Oh speak the Irish language to me
Agus bain dem' chroí an brón
And lift the sorrow from my heart

Ó labhair an teanga Ghaeilge liom
Oh speak the Irish language to me
'Sí teanga cheart na nGael
It's the proper language of the Gaels
An teanga bhinn is ársa 'tá
The sweet most ancient language there is
le fáil ar fud an tsaoil
To be found on the earth

A stór mo chroí is beannacht ort
Delight of my heart blessings on you
A chailín óig gan cháim
Oh young girl without blemish
Cá bhfuil sa saol aon teanga mar
Where in the world is there any language like
Ár dteanga féin le fáil?
Our own language to be found?

Sometimes it helps to think of language as being a door, and one who doesn't know the language cannot access the culture behind the door. I have found this everywhere I've lived. You have a very different experience living in a place where you can connect through language. It not only allows you to show respect, but it also enables you to see things, taste things, learn things and embrace and understand things you wouldn't necessarily be able to without the portal of language.

Maybe a useful way to start is by learning how to say you don't understand:

- **Ní thuigim** /nee HIG-gim/ – I don't understand!
- **Tuigim** /TIG-gim/ – I understand
- **Ní** /nee/ – not. We add a 'h' to make it 'thuigim' and to show it's in the negative form.
- **Abair é liomsa** /OBBer ay LUM-sa/ – say it with me:
- **Ní thuigim** /nee HIG-gim/

Feel those sounds around your mouth. The long **í** /ee/ sound. The **fada** – accent – takes the stress. Then there is stress on the first syllable /HIG-gim/. This is a common feature of Irish which lends to its musicality – the nuances, intonation and rise and fall of the rhythm.

Let's begin with **Ní thuigim** – I don't understand! We can also say **Ní thuigeann mé** /nee HIG-gun may/ in its full form. We must allow for not understanding, and release the self-inflicted pressure of knowing everything or achieving comprehension immediately. For some readers, maybe it's not understanding anything in Irish, and for others it's not understanding the blockage we have with it.

Overwhelm leads to paralysis, inaction and anxiety, but the steady belief that you are capable will see you through. Let's move together towards understanding.

There is a great word in Irish for courage – **misneach**. It is not the warrior-like, storming-the-battle type of courage, but an everyday committed bravery to do what is right. An inexhaustible urge to try, and to be kind with yourself in the attempt. A resilience to believe in starting again, because we can always begin again.

Tá raidhse deiseanna i ngach anáil – There is a cloudburst of possibilities in every breath.

As a learner, and we are all learners, **ní bhíonn rath ach mar a mbíonn smacht** – there does be no success without discipline. **Tada gan iarracht** – nothing without effort.

Putting recently acquired language into use works. It soaks into your brain when you use what you're learning. When you like the sound of a word in this book, find a chance to use it. While repeated exposure can also be a key to unlocking a language, like listening to the radio, podcasts, watching TV or reading the newspaper, there are some techniques that truly help language learning click.

A beginner mindset. An effective method. A motivating community. Accepting and acknowledging that you *can* learn Irish is often much harder than actually learning it.

NOD IONTACH – TOP TIP

Keep a journal of new Irish words and phrases you have learned.
- **Bain triail as!** – Try it out! (literally: extract a trial out of it).
- **Bain taitneamh as!** – Enjoy it! (literally: extract shining out of it).

CLEACHTADH – PRACTICE

An cuimhin leat? – Do you remember? Try to match these Irish phrases with their English translation:

Is fiú agus is féidir	I don't understand
Grá mór	Nothing without effort
Bain taitneamh as	It's worth it and you can do it
Bain triail as	Try it out
Ní thuigim	Enjoy it
Tada gan iarracht	Big love

You'll find the **freagraí** – answers to this exercise at the end of the book.

3

An Teanga Atá i gCeist
The Language in Question

We use the phrase **i gceist** – in question – a lot in Irish, and also in Hiberno-English, the version of English we speak in Ireland. The man in question, the matter in question, the ingredient in question. Curiously, it doesn't apply to something we are *questioning*, rather a fact or a state that is being discussed. The word **ceist** – question – is a feminine noun, **an cheist**, from Old Irish **ceist**, from the Latin *quaestiō*.

The 'language question' in the context of Ireland refers to debates and issues surrounding the use, preservation and promotion of **an Ghaeilge**. It is a multifaceted issue tied to culture, identity, politics and history.

A native language holds the soul and memory of its people. Just as the Irish language offers insight into an indigenous way of thinking, it also opens a portal to a different way of being. What power and wisdom can be found for the problems we face today through reconnecting with our indigenous language? What healing and problem-solving might lie in it? To gain a better understanding of this, we need to first connect ourselves to the story of the decline of Irish, a language once spoken throughout our island.

Stair na Gaeilge – A History of Irish

An Ghaeilge is an Indo-European language, about a millennium older than English. With a strong oral tradition passed down by word of mouth through **filí** – poets, **seanchaithe** – storytellers, and **draoithe** – druids, it has the oldest vernacular literature in western Europe. The textured and playful way the Irish use words, even in Hiberno-English, has created a rich literary scene and Ireland is renowned for producing world-class authors, poets and playwrights.

The earliest inscriptions in Ogham script (4th–6th century AD) provide the first written evidence of Irish. Ogham is an early medieval alphabet used primarily to write the Irish language. It consists of a series of notches and lines carved into stone, wood or metal, typically along the edge of a surface. The inscriptions were written vertically, and it is thought that they were used to record names and tribal affiliations, which served to indicate land ownership. About 400 inscribed stone pillars or 'standing stones', as they are known, still exist today. The majority of these are found in County Kerry, Wales, Scotland, England, the Isle of Man, France and Spain.

Old Irish evolved into Modern Irish, Scottish Gaelic and Manx. These three Gaelic languages, along with their Celtic cousins – Welsh, Cornish and Breton – make up the surviving six Celtic languages.

Ireland's pre-colonial culture was imbued with nature, spirituality, community and oral tradition. Irish was the dominant language of the island. The Proto-Celtic word *weidus* gave us the word **Gael** meaning 'Irish person', but derives from the idea 'of the wild' or 'of the woods'. Indeed, most of Ireland was covered in forests, and Ireland's non-punitive legal system, the Brehon Laws, showed a focus on compensation, social harmony and environmental protection. It was a highly structured society, one that was spiritually connected to the land.

British colonisation of Ireland began in earnest during the late 12th century with the Norman invasion of Ireland

in 1169. It was initiated by Strongbow – Richard de Clare –
and sanctioned by King Henry II of England. This marked
the start of sustained English involvement in Irish affairs.
Ireland was the first colonised territory of the British
Empire. With this came the hallmark of every country
under occupation: a deliberate and systematic destruction
of the indigenous culture and language by the coloniser. As
Kenyan author Ngũgĩ wa Thiong'o wrote in his seminal book
Decolonising the Mind (1986), 'The bullet was the means of
the physical subjugation. Language was the means of the
spiritual subjugation'. Ngũgĩ argued that language is the
collective memory bank of a people's experience in history; it's
not just a means of communication, but a carrier of culture.
What if your very thinking, your psyche, were preserved
within your butchered tongue? Hozier's song, *Butchered
Tongue*, explores what decolonising the Gaelic psyche
means, and how life continues in a land so deeply marked
by interference and injustice. His work confronts colonial
violence like pitch capping and the 1798 Wexford Rebellion.
Despite the suppression of their native language, the Irish
remained defiant and resilient against their attackers.

In the article 'Rewriting Cromwell: A Case of Deafening
Silences' in the Canadian Journal of History, historian John
Morrill describes the Cromwellian conquest of Ireland in
the mid-17th century as the 'greatest exercise of ethnic

cleansing of early modern Europe'. Under the leadership of Oliver Cromwell, the English Parliamentary forces implemented policies that led to significant displacement and suffering among the Irish Catholic population. **Staraithe** – historians, such as Mark Levene and Alan Axelrod, have characterised these actions as ethnic cleansing, aiming to remove Irish Catholics from the eastern part of the country. Others, like Tim Pat Coogan, have gone further, describing Cromwell's actions as **cinedhíothach** – genocidal.

During British rule, particularly after the 17th century, the English language gradually replaced Irish due to policies like land confiscation, the Penal Laws, and the introduction of English as the language of government, education and commerce. People who've come through the Irish school system often hold the belief that Irish was 'beaten into us'. And sadly, there is truth in this for many. But predating it is another sad fact: English was beaten into us first, while the Irish was beaten out of us. In 1831, a state system of education was introduced with one of the main aims being to teach English to Irish children. The **bata scóir** – score stick – was used to punish children caught speaking their native language. The **bata** was tied with a string around a child's neck, and a notch was carved into the stick every time they spoke Irish. At the end of the day, the child was beaten according to how many notches they had.

The Irish-speaking populations were further decimated by **An Gorta Mór** – The Great Famine (1845–52). Charles Trevelyan, a British civil servant in charge of famine relief, is often quoted as saying the famine was a 'direct stroke of an all-wise and all-merciful Providence' that was meant to teach the Irish a lesson. About a million people died and over a million emigrated, reducing the population by 25%, making Ireland the only country in the world with a lower population now than it had 180 years ago. The west of Ireland, where native speakers felt the brunt of transplantation policies, poverty, starvation and emigration, was hit the hardest.

The Irish language came to be seen as backwards and embarrassing. Irish people learned to internalise a shame around the very language that builds our humour, our tenderness, our way of seeing the world. Have you heard the subtle insult of something being 'so Irish'? Having midnight mass at 6pm? So Irish. Bringing your own milk on holidays? So Irish! There's something uneasy, a little queasy about it.

Yet in truth nothing about any language or culture is backwards or nonsensical. Before healing must come understanding. When an indigenous culture is dismantled, destroyed, denied, suppressed and shamed, it does not come out unscathed. A sense of shame is inherent in that scar.

A paradigm shift, necessary for us to value our indigenous language, is to become aware that our native language – which predates colonisation, Christianity and capitalism – is bursting with poetry, learning, soul and wisdom.

Over the centuries the language has faced the Norman invasion, the Statutes of Kilkenny, the plantations, the Penal Laws, **an drochshaol** ('the bad life' of the Famine) an ethnocide and ecocide – some might say genocide – and an ongoing identity crisis. Despite the many struggles, Irish is a survivor, just like its people.

Níl sí marbh – she's not dead, **tá sí marfach** – she's deadly!

NOD IONTACH – TOP TIP

Speaking of poetry, Irish-language poets have long enriched our artistic culture and have been celebrated both at home and abroad. Check out the poetry of Colm Breathnach, Antoine Ó Raifteirí and Áine Durkin to name but a few.

Athbheochan na Gaeilge – The Gaelic Revival

In the late 19th and early 20th centuries, the Irish Literary Revival and organisations like **Conradh na Gaeilge** – The Gaelic League – sought to revitalise the language by setting up classes and summer programs, and promoting Irish in the arts. It inspired key figures of the 1916 Easter Rising such as Pádraig Pearse and Eoin MacNeill, who were active members of the League. Irish became a symbol of national identity and resistance against colonialism. The Gaelic Revival was the cultural foundation for a political revolution and paved the road to independence. In 1901, the Municipal Council of Dublin began installing bilingual street signs featuring both Irish and English names, reflecting the Gaelic Revival movement. In 1937, the Irish Constitution declared Irish as the first official language, with English as the second. The state was committed to promoting Irish, especially in education and government.

The Gaeltacht regions, where Irish remained the vernacular language, were seen as authentic remnants of Ireland's pre-colonial past. They offered a direct connection to the linguistic and cultural heritage that the revivalists sought to restore. The Gaeltacht areas are traditionally on the west and north coast in places like **Contae Chiarraí** –

County Kerry, **Contae Chorcaí** – County Cork, **Contae na Gaillimhe** – County Galway, **Contae Mhaigh Eo** – County Mayo, **Contae Dhún na nGall** – County Donegal, and also **Contae na Mí** – County Meath and **Contae Phort Láirge** – County Waterford.

An lá atá inniu ann – Nowadays (the day that's in it today)

This revival movement, which inspired generations of Irish people to strive for independence and a reconnection to cultural roots, has carried on through the generations. Now we see that the reticence to learn our language is changing. We have urban Gaeltachts flourishing in places like inner-city **Béal Feirste** – Belfast, the commuter towns of **Baile Átha Cliath** – Dublin, **Luimneach** – Limerick, and **Doire** – Derry. Neighbourhoods not traditionally known as Irish-speaking are embracing our culture and living the language, feeling the sense of community and togetherness it fosters, and enjoying the benefits. There are resettlement schemes to incentivise families to move to Gaeltacht areas, and there are grants available to stay, study and create in the Gaeltacht.

Activist grassroots groups like An Dream Dearg have campaigned powerfully for language rights in the north of Ireland. Cultúrlann McAdam Ó Fiaich, a major Irish-language cultural centre on the Falls Road in Belfast, has become a hub for events, education and social life. Areas such as Clondalkin, Lucan, and Rathfarnham in Dublin have seen the rise of urban Irish-speaking networks, supported by **Gaelscoileanna** – Irish-medium schools. These communities are driving the language forward, creating Irish-speaking spaces in workplaces, universities, social media, music and even politics. They are inclusive and forward-thinking, understand that language rights are human rights, and are vocal about other humanitarian crises currently occurring around the world.

We are experiencing not so much a cultural wave at this point in time, but a flood of awakened and enlightened thought. And not just thought, but **gníomhú** – action.

Ní siombail í labhairt na Gaeilge don oidhreacht agus don bhféiniúlacht, is gníomh oidhreachta agus féiniúlachta í – Speaking Irish is not a symbol of heritage and identity, it is an act of heritage and identity.

The last Gaelic revival was about recovering what was lost due to the famine and colonisation. This burgeoning

Gaelic revival is about celebrating, reclaiming and working through the pain of it. From survival to revival.

The Official Languages Act of 2003 ensures Government departments must provide services through both Irish and English. Irish versions of **pasanna** – passports, tax forms, and legal documents must be made available. There is also the option of doing your driving test through Irish, although complaints have been made that these provisions are not suitably adhered to. A 2021 amendment set a 20% Irish-speaking recruitment target for public service jobs by 2030.

Foras na Gaeilge, the body responsible for the promotion of the Irish language throughout the island of Ireland, supports Irish journalism, online content, and publishing. They create approximately 2,000 to 3,000 new Irish words annually, averaging about 250 new terms each month. These terms are developed to address emerging concepts and technologies, ensuring the Irish language remains current and comprehensive. We see words emerging like **Breatimeacht** – a term coined for Brexit, combining **Breatain** – Britain and **imeacht** – exit. Irish has been an Official Language of the European Union since 2007, and has full working language status in the EU since 2022.

This means that all laws, documents, and debates are translated into Irish and there is an increased demand for Irish-speaking **aistritheoirí** – translators and **ateangairí** – interpreters.

There has been growth in Irish-language media, such as the national Irish-language television channel, **TG4**, and radio station, **Raidió na Gaeltachta**. Digital tools and apps for learning Irish have also gained popularity. Social media has democratised the language by making it more accessible and contemporary, and publishing content readily available for users to engage with the language. We see pages focused on food and fashion, travel and music, making it interesting, creative and authentic, and creating new communities of speakers who have opportunities to use what they're learning.

Now, what we're experiencing is a proliferation of Irish-made, quality productions like *Kneecap*, *Crá*, *Love/Hate*, and *Bad Sisters*. Young people drink pints of Guinness or Beamish and wear tweed caps. We are living in an Ireland more comfortable with its place in the world. In my lifetime alone, Ireland has voted Yes to divorce, same-sex marriage and access to abortion and has enacted the world's first smoking ban. And this from a country where, for many years, there was little separation between Church and State.

It is only natural that change occurs and societies transform. But in Ireland, it feels like there is a pulsating cultural shift in the reclamation of our identity through language. 'It has created a generation of hibernophiles', writes Kelly Earley in the article, 'Accidentally Irish: How Ruining the Economy Made Us All Irish Again'.

Some people sparking this connection with Irish include:

- David Keoghan, who is unearthing the lost Celtic sport of **tógáil cloch** – stone-lifting.
- Biird and Lisa Canny are lilting their way to *The Late Late Show* and injecting a dynamic and fresh zest into **ceol traidisiúnta na hÉireann** – traditional Irish music.
- Davy Holden is teaching **blúiríní soláimhsithe de cheachtanna staire** – manageable nuggets of Irish history lessons on TikTok and Instagram.
- Madelyn Monaghan is **ag caoineadh** – keening in the original **sean-nós** – old style from New York.
- Irish-language content creators are scattered **timpeall an domhain** – around the world.
- Dian Killian is **ag scríobh** – writing on Substack about the liminality of Irish and how our language can save the world.

- Morgan Bullock is the first Black Riverdance **damhsóir Gaelach** – Irish dancer.
- Irish language comedy shows are being put on by **fuirseoirí** – comedians Áine Gallagher, Julie Jay and Martin Angolo.
- **Scannáin uafáis** – horror films in Irish, like *Fréwaka* by Aislinn Clarke are hitting our screens.
- **Stáiseanóireacht álainn** – beautiful stationery is being produced with **nathanna Gaeilge** – Irish phrases by Rachel Corcoran and Prints of Ireland.
- Fashion designers Pellador, De Búrca (@deburcadesign) and Aoife Cawley are emblazoning Irishness onto wearable signifiers of identity.
- We're hearing musicians like Hozier, Dermot Kennedy, Le Boom, Fontaines D.C., Cushla and Amano introducing Irish lyrics and sounds to their music.
- Yoga le Naoise is creating yoga classes through Irish and wellness events with her brand **Tabhair Aire** – Take Care.
- Ciara Ní É, the poet, presenter and filmmaker founded REIC, a bilingual spoken word event and co-founded the LGBTQ+ arts collective AerachAiteachGaelach. Her play *Grindr, Saghdar agus Cher* and short film *Claonadh* elevate the

language and offer it a provocative and enticing stage in contemporary Ireland.

- Tristan Rosenstock's children's book *Inis Mara* offers a gripping adventure story about climate action, and www.myirishbooks.ie is inspiring a new generation with Irish songs and stories.

Social media is no stranger to the revival of Irish either, and 'Gaeltok' is the name aptly given to the influx of Irish language creators on the app TikTok, a fine example of **imeartas focal** – a pun or play on words – on 'Gaeltacht'. What is so important about this surge is that it shows young people not just sharing content about their language, but proudly living it. Followers feel motivated to learn and are incentivised **snas a chur ar a gcuid Gaeilge** – to put polish on their Irish – in order to understand jokes and references.

Some of my favourite accounts to follow include:
- @Gaelscoilis
- @Gael2GO
- @seanohaodha1
- @joshuascottdavis
- @Gaeilge_bheo

These accounts are gamifying Gaeilge by encouraging more curiosity about our language. They might feature a 'day in the life', where bilingual subtitles and catchy music allay the viewer's anxiety about not knowing every word. They present unboxing videos from Irish clothing brands like Fukil or Fada Jewellery, enacting seemingly innocuous gestures that tap into our subconscious to see how Irish is being spoken, celebrated and promoted. Witnessing young people engaging positively with our language and garnering thousands or millions of views online is pivotal for the language movement.

Ireland today is a multicultural society, and speaking different languages is more commonly part of everyday life. The Irish, well known for emigrating and travelling, are realising, 'Hey, I speak Japanese and German and I don't speak my own language?!' Or maybe they're dating someone from Serbia and who is curious about that road sign, or this brand name, and find themselves saying 'Well, that's Gaeilge, **ár dteanga oifigiúil** – our official language.' **Tosaíonn bród ag fás** – a pride starts to grow.

You will hear the **cogar** – whisper – of **an domhan istigh sna focail** – the world within the words. Pick up a stone and uncover the wonder that lies there. It might not be obvious at first glance, but this is an invitation to root yourself in the language and rather than memorise lumps of letters at surface value, to connect with it.

Over 100 years after fighting for our **saoirse** – freedom – and **neamhspleáchas** – independence, it is still unusual to speak our own language.

Is it possible to rethink, revitalise and relearn? Of course, it is. And it won't even take as long as you think, or as much effort. The Hebrew language was revived. The Māori language *te reo*, Welsh, Manx and Basque have all been rejuvenated successfully. We make up excuses. But, as Irish tells us, an excuse is just a **leithscéal** – a half story.

Ultimately, the language question reflects Ireland's ongoing negotiation with its historical identity, cultural heritage and place in a globalised world. It's time to undo the damage of generations, kindle the fire, and start seeing this gift with fresh eyes.

NOD IONTACH – TOP TIP

Every conversation you have is an opportunity to speak **as Gaeilge**, even just a word or two shared with another person could inspire them to learn or relearn the language and share with more people. Spark that flame for other people.

CLEACHTADH – PRACTICE

Associating new words with something you already know is a powerful and effective technique to anchor them in your memory. Here are five words from this chapter and a hint to help you remember them. Get creative with other words; connect the word with something visual, a wacky sound, or a feeling the word evokes in you.

Soon you'll have a **stór focal** – a treasury of words, a vocabulary.

- **Ceist** /kesht/ – question. Think of how it sounds like 'quest'; you're on a quest for knowledge!
- **Teanga** /chonga/ – language/tongue. Think of the sound of it, musical, like dancing in a conga line. You might think – nothing is wronga with my **teanga**, focusing on your tongue and the sounds and language it produces.
- **Pas** /poss/ – passport; **pasanna** /POSS-anna/ –

passports. Think of how this document helps you 'pass' from one place to another.

- **Ceol** /kyole/ – music. It almost sounds like 'key-hole' when you slow it down, and music is inviting you through the keyhole sometimes in a rural Irish pub.
- **Saoirse** /SEE-er-sha/ – freedom, also a girl's name. The sea feels free to me, then you could imagine sea shells and say those two sounds /s/ and /sh/ together a few times.

4

Tríocha Trí is a Tríú
'Tirty Tree and a Turd'

A student of mine recounted his experience riding the Luas. At each stop, he heard a recorded lady's voice announcing the place name, first in Irish followed by the English. He said, 'The beauty of Irish flowed from her lips as smoothly as a Guinness goes down'. His words struck me. I thought that sentiment was just lovely. He continued:

> 'In my mind was a question. How do these folks make the language sound so cool from that jumble of letters they use? Even at 80 years of age, I'm beginning to find out from your course, Mollie. Your teaching method is unlocking the mystery for me and for that "**go raibh maith agat**" – thank you.'

This student's sentiment is reflective of a common refrain that Irish doesn't look the way it sounds. However, a friend and student of mine was studying on his laptop in the United States and a Ukrainian barman caught a glimpse of a lesson where I was explaining prefixes. The prefix 'in-' means '-able':

- **Inchaite** /in-KKOT-cheh/ – wearable
- **Inite** /in-ITCH-eh/ – edible
- **Inchreidte** /in-KKRET-cheh/ – plausible, believable
- **Indéanta** /in-JAY-in-ta/– possible, doable
- **Inlasta** /in-LOSS-ta/ – flammable

Your man, the Ukrainian, read all of them out correctly. My friend joked, 'What does that tell you? Irish is not that hard for non-native English speakers to pronounce! English is the problem, **a chara!**' – my friend.

This reminded me of a young Ukrainian boy who featured on Irish TV recently. Misha Yerhidzé, who fled the war in Ukraine with his family and settled in Baile an Fheirtéaraigh in County Kerry, has fully embraced the Irish language and culture. Fair play to ya, Misha. **Maith thú!** – Good on you! He has learned Irish to fluency in just six months, through immersion at school and in the community, music lessons and new friendships. I love how

Misha can introduce himself – **Is mise Misha** /iss misha misha/ – I am Misha.

Since I started teaching Irish, I've been impressed with the mindset of those coming to it with a fresh attitude and an openness to the language, which invites more absorption. There is a natural love and familiarity with the language, even in those who have no ancestral ties to Ireland, and the ease with which some students can get their tongue around our Celtic *teanga* – language is incredible. Some learners might suggest that Irish orthography and pronunciation are designed to act as a code language, to trick and distract our colonising neighbours, and to make it difficult to understand. Think of it like choreography – you can't learn a full dance by just thinking about it; you must move your body and practice before the muscles will remember it. If you can start speaking, soon your mouth will catch up to your brain, and the words will come to you and flow out of you.

If we are thwarted in our efforts by the strict and irregular rules of the English language, if we look at Irish script and expect English sounds, if we force English onto Irish, we will confuse ourselves and retreat. We will fear the language that seems so incoherent and intangible, we will reduce its value and deem it unnecessary, a time–waster. It will mock us with its difficulty and remind us how detached we are, and how worthless we are, once again instilling that shame that colonisation thrives on.

Keeping in mind it is a bit outrageous to spell one language using another, or to assume that all Irish speakers sound the same: the pronunciations in my guide are approximations. Of course, accents are not the same in all regions, and people pronounce words slightly differently. The sound of ó or á, for example, can vary by region throughout Ireland and the person speaking.

Jerry Kelly of the Philo-Celtic Society says that there are as many dialects as speakers of the language. This rings true, and its truth breaks through layers of hesitation, confusion and self-imposed feelings of inadequacy. We can feel that we want to be 100% accurate and eloquent, but there is a necessary open-armed vulnerability that needs to occur to embrace anything.

I teach the Official Standard in terms of grammar and spelling, and my own accent is a mix of Munster and Connacht. I cover all dialects in my courses. Generally, I prefer not to use phonemes in my teaching because I think it deadens the music of the language, thus the meaning of the words. We don't need to 'simplify' Irish or create a spelling system that looks more like it sounds; I believe we've already got the perfect one. However, for guidance and ease of reference, I've included phonemes below.

Cleachtadh Fuaimnithe – Pronunciation Practice

Note: Word stress is usually on the first syllable, unless there is a **fada** (accent over vowels) in the word.

Gutaí – *Vowels*

	Fuaimniú – Sounds like:	Mar shampla – For Example:
a	'o' in the English word 'clock'	**cat** /kot/ – cat
o	'u' in the English word 'bull'	**nod** /nud/ – hint
u	'u' in the English word 'bull'	**muc** /muk/ – pig
i	'i' in the English word 'fish'	**im** /im/ – butter
e	'e' in the English word 'met	**file** /FILL-eh/ – poet

An Síneadh Fada – *The Long Stretch*

Fada means 'long'. The 'fada' shows that the vowel sound is elongated. It's sometimes called the **síneadh fada** – long stretch. It is the only accent in Modern Irish. The **fada** is a diacritic mark that only appears over vowels. It looks like this: á Á ó Ó ú Ú í Í é É.

	Fuaimniú – Sounds like:	**Mar shampla – For Example:**
á	/aw/ in the English word 'law'	**grá** /graw/ – love
ó	like /oh/ in the English word 'phone'	**bó** /boh/ – cow
ú	/oo/ in the English word 'zoo'	**sú** /soo/ – juice
í	/ee/ in the English word 'key'	**rís** /reesh/ – rice
é	/ay/ in the English word 'bay'	**sé** /shay/ – he/it

Déanann an fada difear mór! – The fada makes all the difference

A **fada** on a vowel can be a big deal. Here are some examples of words that have a different meaning when a 'fada' is included:

ait /atch/ – weird	**áit** /awtch/ – place
briste /BRISH-teh/ – broken	**bríste** /BREESH-teh/ – trousers
caca /KA-ka/ – poo	**cáca** /KAW-ka/ – cake
mala /MOLL-ah/ – eyebrow	**mála** /MAW-la/ – bag
sean /shan/ – old	**Seán** /shawn/ – Seán (male name)
lagar /LOGG-ar/ – faintness, weakness	**lágar** /LAW-gar/ – lager
ciste /KISH-tch/ – fund	**císte** /KEESH-teh/ – cake
te /cheh/ – hot	**té** /chay/ – person
snamh /snov/ – dislike	**snámh** /snawv/ – swim
bradán /brod-AWN/ – salmon	**brádán** /braw-dawn/ – drizzle

Fuaimeanna na gConsan – *Consonant sounds*

The following letters do not appear in the alphabet of the Irish language: J, K, Q, V, W, X, Y, Z. Some of these letters may appear in new words or words borrowed from other languages.

- Consonant sounds can be broad or slender depending on the closest vowel:
  - Broad vowels: A, O and U
  - Slender vowels: I and E

	Fuaimniú – Sounds like:	Mar shampla – For Example:
b	/b/ in 'bag'	**béal** /BAY-el/ – mouth
c	/k/ in 'Coca Cola'	**croí** /kree/ – heart
d – broad	/th/ or /ð/ in 'brother'	**doras** /ðUR-ris/– door
d – slender	/j/ in 'juice'	**deoch** /jukk/ – drink
f	/f/ in 'forget'	**fáinne** /FAWN-ye/– ring

g	/g/ in 'go'	**gairdín** /gar-jeen/ – garden
h	/h/ in 'hit'	**hata** /HOTta/ – hat
l – broad	/l/ in 'law'	**lón** /lone/ – lunch
l – slender	/l/ in 'million'	**leabhar** /LYAU-wer/ – book
m	/m/ in 'men'	**mála** /MAW-la/ – bag
n	/n/ in 'never'	**nasc** /nosk/ – link
p	/p/ in 'pen'	**post** /pust/ – job
r – broad	/r/ in 'right'	**rún** / roon / – secret
r – slender	/zh/ sound in 'leisure'	**réalta** /hRAY-alta/ – star
s – broad	/s/ in 'soul'	**solas** /SULL-us/ – light
s – slender	/sh/ in 'sugar'	**siúcra** / SHYOO-kra / – sugar
t – broad	/t/ in 'tear'	**tae** /tay/ – tea
t – slender	/ch/ in 'church'	**teach** /chokk/ – house

Fuaimeanna an tSéimhithe – *'Séimhiú' sounds (lenition)*

The way we say 'th' in Ireland has been mocked since the beginning of colonisation. We pronounce 'th' as /h/ in Irish. We hop over the th. It is breathy – a short, sharp exhale. It is a spirant. For example, **a hathair** /a HAH-herzh/ – her father or **máthair** /MAW-herhz/ – mother. The way that people sometimes complain how Irish doesn't sound how it looks … just imagine being Irish and speaking Irish. You start to speak English, completely new to the language, and someone is telling you that what looks like /h/ to you instead sounds like /θ/ (the unvoiced 'th', as in 'moth') or /ð/ (the voiced 'th', as in 'mother'). While it can be difficult to master new sounds, with practice we can learn how they work.

The **séimhiú** (addition of 'h' after a consonant) is also known as lenition in English. **'Séimh'** means 'smooth' and lenition smoothens the sound of a consonant. The 'séimhiú' is a feature that serves to aid the ease and flow of speech.

The **séimhiú** can go on these 9 letters:
- b (bh, Bh)
- c (ch, Ch)
- d (dh, Dh)
- f (fh, Fh)

- g (gh, Gh)
- m (mh, Mh)
- p (ph, Ph)
- s (sh, Sh)
- t (th, Th)

You might remember these 9 consonants – B, C, D, F, G, M, P, S, T – with the mnemonic:

Be careful, don't forget: good Mollie put **séimhiú** there!

It doesn't affect L, N, or R (Think: Eleanor), and it doesn't affect the combined consonants SC, SM, SP, ST (Think: **Sc**allions **Sm**ell **Sp**icy in **St**ew.)

FÍRIC FHÁNACH – FUN FACT

Hebrew, Finnish and Russian exhibit some consonant changes similar to lenition, but the Celtic languages (Irish, Scottish Gaelic, and Manx) have the most systematic and pervasive systems of initial consonant mutations.

'Séimhiú' sounds can be broad or slender depending on the closest vowel.

	Fuaimniú – Sounds like:	Mar shampla – For Example:
bh – broad	/w/ in 'win'	**mo bhus** /muh wus/ – my bus
bh – broad	/v/ if it is before or after a 'long sound' like a **fada** or a similarly long sound	**lámha** /LAW-va/ – hands or **liamhás** / lee-ah-vaws/ – ham
bh – slender	/v/ in 'vase'	**mo bheoir** /muh vyor/ – my beer
bh	We will hear more /v/ sounds in Munster and more /w/ sounds in Connacht and Ulster for bh and mh.	
bh – word end	bh at the end of a word sounds like /v/, as in 'of'	**dubh** /ðuv/ – black
ch	/kk/ in the German word 'achtung', very like 'ch' or 'g' in Dutch	**ach** /okk/ – but

dh – broad	/g/ in 'grim' but a little throatier	**Dhúisigh mé** /GOO-shig may/ – I woke up
dh – slender	/y/ in 'yes'	**Dheisigh mé** /YESH-ig may/ – I fixed
fh	silent	**an fhuinneog** / onn IN-yoge/ – the window
gh	/gg/ – very guttural	**Ghlan sí** /gglon shee/ – She cleaned
mh – broad	/w/ in 'win'	**mo mhála** /muh WAW-la/ – my bag
mh slender	/v/ in 'vase'	**mo mhic** /muh vik/ – my sons
mh – word end	More /v/ in Connacht and Munster, and /w/ in Ulster	**lámh** /lawv/ – hand
ph	'ph' in 'phone' and 'photo'	**Phós sé** /fose shay/ – He married
sh	/h/ in 'hit'	**Shiúil mé** /hyool may/ – I walked
th	/h/ in 'hit'	**Thit mé** /hit may/ – I fell

Bring back those **poncanna buailte** (∵), says you! The **ponc buailte** – struck/hit point in older Irish lettering showed that the consonant was affected by lenition. Also known as the **ponc séimhithe** – softening dot, it was used to indicate lenition before it was replaced with 'h'.

Examples in **Cló Gaelach** Irish font vs. Modern Irish:

- **ᴀʀ ṡᴇ́ᴀɴ** → ar Sheán – on Seán
- **ɪᴀʀᴛᴀʀ ċᴏɴɴᴀċᴛ** → Iarthar Chonnacht – West Connacht
- **ʟᴀ́ ḟᴇ́ɪʟᴇ ʙʀı́ᴆᴇ** → Lá Fhéile Bríde – St. Brigid's Day

The dots above the **séimhiú** letters were so gorgeous, but here we are now with our beloved 'h'.

The **séimhiú** is used in various situations, including:
- Counting things 2 to 6 (**dhá bhád** – two boats, **trí pheann** – three pens, **ceithre sheomra** – four rooms, **cúig gheansaí** – five jumpers, **sé ghairdín** – six gardens),
- Possession: my, your and his (**mo mhadra** – my dog, **do chat** – your cat, **a theach** – his house),
- Feminine nouns beginning with a suitable consonant following the article 'the' (**an bhean** –

the woman, **an fharraige** – the sea, **an phóg** – the kiss),

- Verbs that start with a suitable consonant, in the past and conditional tenses (**Dhún mé** – I closed, **Cheannóinn** – I would buy),
- Negative form of verbs across the tenses (**Ní thuigim** – I don't understand, **Ní bheidh mé** – I will not be, **Ní cheannóinn** – I would not buy).

The Urú – Eclipsis

The '**urú**' is a grammatical feature also known as 'eclipsis'. One letter eclipses – or covers – another. It comes from the Old Irish **airdubad**. This used to be spelled '**urdhubhadh**' before standardisation of Irish spelling in the 20th century – '**ur**' meaning 'fore' and '**dubhadh**' meaning 'blackening'. Just as the moon eclipses the sun, one sound eclipses or covers the sound after it. It happens for various reasons, but similarly to its cousin, the '**séimhiú**' (which softens), the 'urú' is all about aiding the ease and flow of speech. The **urú** creates a fairly nasal sound.

The '**urú**' goes on 7 consonants and is always in lower case:
- B (mB, mb)
- C (gC, gc)

- D (nD, nd)
- F (bhF, bhf)
- G (nG, ng)
- P (bP, bp)
- T (dT, dt)

One way to remember them is:

My brother got caught not doing dishes tonight. Nobody gets blueberry pie before he finishes:
mB, gC, nD, dT, nG, bP, bhF.

The first letter eclipses the second, so we only hear the first letter. mB sounds like /m/, gC sounds like /g/, nD sounds like /n/ and so on … well, nG sounds like /ŋ/. This is a nasal sound made in the same position as /k/ and /g/, so the tongue is raised at the back, touching the soft palate. It is the sound we hear in the English words ending with 'ing'.

We employ the **urú** for various reasons, like with the preposition '**i**' (in), when we say where we live, **Tá mé i mo chónaí** – I am in my living – **i mBaile Átha Cliath** – in the town of the hurdled ford (Dublin). **Baile** is town, but changes to **mBaile** after the preposition '**i**'.

	Fuaimniú – Sounds like	Mar shampla – For Example:
mB	/m/	**i mBostún** /ih MUS-toon/ – in Boston
gC	/g/	**i gCorcaigh** /ih GURK-ig/ – in Cork
nD	/n/	**i nDoire** /ih NUR-reh/ – in Derry
dT	/d/	**i dTiobraid Árann** /ih DIB-rid OR-in/ – in Tipperary
nG	/ŋ/	**i nGaillimh** /ih ŋGOL-yiv/ – in Galway
bP	/b/	**i bPáras** /ih BAWR-us/ – in Paris
bhF	/v/	**i bhFear Manach** /ih var MON-okk/ – in Fermanagh

Cá bhfuil tú i do chónaí? /kaw wil too ih duh kkoh–nee/ – Where are you in your living? Where do you live?

We use the **urú**:
- to clarify ownership with possessive adjectives:

ár mbus our bus, **bhur ndeartháir** your (plural) brother, **a gcat** – their cat, **a n–árasán** – their apartment.

- to count things 7–10: **seacht gcnoc** – 7 hills, **ocht n–oíche** – 8 nights, **naoi dtraein** – 9 trains, **deich ngabha**r – 10 goats (notice how we use **n**- on vowels if an **urú** is invited).
- in reported speech, on the verb in relative clauses and questions using 'that': **Chuala mé nach ndéanann sí faic** – I heard that she doesn't do anything/doesn't do nothing (double negatives are ok in Irish).

The **urú** is a mutation, an addition that is made to make the language flow more freely out of our mouth. Take, for example, the question form in the Present or Future tense. It starts with 'An'. 'An' is a question marker. Pronounced /on/, the sound is softer than the English word 'on'. The tongue flattens and opens the teeth slightly with the /n/ sound, as if you are about to say 'on the' but you get cut off or interrupted before you can say 'the'.

Say it now a couple of times to feel how the tongue positions itself lightly resting on the upper ridge behind the top teeth.

- **Dún** – to close. **An ndúnann tú?** – Do you close?
- **Glan** – to clean. **An nglanann tú?** – Do you clean?
- **Téigh** – to go. **An dtéann tú?** – Do you go?
- **Cuir** – to put. **An gcuireann tú?** – Do you put?
- **Nach** is the negative question particle, meaning 'Don't'
    - **Nach ndéanann tú caife sa bhaile?** – Don't you make coffee at home?

Notice how the verb takes the 'urú' and an ending ('ann' if it's broad, and '-eann' if it's slender when they're short verbs (one syllable).

If the verb is long (two syllables) we will add '-aíonn' for broad verbs and '-íonn' for slender verbs. I teach these endings by introducing a fictional couple called Ann and Ian. These endings -(e)ann and -(a)íonn sound somewhat like the names Ann and Ian.

- **Ceannaigh** – to buy. **An gceannaíonn tú?** – Do you buy?
- **Deisigh** – to fix. **An ndeisíonn tú?** – Do you fix?
- **Codail** – to sleep. **Nach gcodlaíonn tú go maith?** – Don't you sleep well?

The beauty of the 'séimhiú' and 'urú' mutations is that we can still see the original spelling hidden in the word. For example, we see **páistí** children, in the words **a páistí** /ah pawshtee/ – her children; **a pháistí** /ah fawshtee/ – his children; **a bpáistí** /ah bawshtee/ – their children. We eclipse the letter with another, but we don't remove it, so we can see that while it changes sound and spelling, the Latin alphabet used to house our 33 consonant sounds is working overtime. Letters can make multiple sounds, as we see with broad or slender vowels. Latin has about 20 consonants. Irish was more of a spoken language when Christianity came to Ireland, and the monks transcribing manuscripts used the alphabet they were used to – Latin. This is why people often remark that Irish isn't pronounced as it 'should' be pronounced. When we look at words expecting English sounds or spellings, it can be confusing. It is, after all, a different language.

A student asked me once, 'Why the *séimhiús* and the *urús*?' Like, what's the point of it all?

It's a brilliant question, which is asked all too rarely. Why this initial mutation? The main reason is for ease and flow of speech. Isn't it easier to say '**an bhean**' (the woman) than 'an bean'?

The lips only need to close once. Same goes with '**mo mhadra**' (my dog) and 'mo madra'. Speech is uninterrupted.

Sometimes the **séimhiú** or **urú** is used to differentiate meaning, for example:

- **A chat** – his cat. We add a **séimhiú** to consonants for 'his' and nothing to vowels, e.g. **a úll** – his apple.
- **A cat** – her cat. We add nothing to consonants for 'her', and 'h' to vowels, e.g. **a húll** – her apple.
- **A gcat** – their cat. We add an **urú** before a consonant after 'their', and 'n-' to vowels, e.g. **a n-úll** – their apple.

Words mutate in accordance with their function. These mutations which occur at the beginning of a word with lenition, or at the end of a word with a suffix, highlight a rootedness which helps you find your way back. **Dochreidte!** Unbelievable! A student of mine was learning about prefixes. He could see after the lesson how **do-** = un-, **creid** = believe, and **-te** the adjectival form built the word **Dochreidte!** – Unbelievable!

Here are vowel cluster sounds:

	Fuaimniú – Sounds like:	Mar shampla – For Example:
aoi	/ee/ in 'fee', 'key'	**saoirse** /see-er-sha/ – freedom
ae	/ay/ in 'air', 'age'	**aerfort** /air-furt/ – airport
ai	/a/ in 'cat', 'band'	**aisling** /ash-ling/ – dream
ao	/ee/ or /ay/	**saol** /seel/ or /sail/ – life
ei	/e/ in 'met'	**eitleán** /etch-lawn/ – airplane
ea	/a/ in 'cat'	**meas** /mass/ – respect
eo	/yo/	**beo** /byo/ – alive
ia	/EE-ya/ as in 'see ya!'	**bia** /BEE-ya/ – food
io	/u/ in 'bull'	**ionad** /UN-ud/ – centre
	/ee/ in 'teeth'	**iontach** /EEN-tokk/ – great
	/oo/ (Munster Irish)	**iontach** /OON-tokk/ – great
oi	/i/ in 'fish'	**oiriúnach** /ir-OON-okk/ – suitable
ua	/OO-wa/	**uachtar** /OO-wakk-tar/ – cream
ui	/i/ in 'fish'	**uisce** /ISH-ka/ – water

CLEACHTADH – PRACTICE

Conas a déarfá na focail seo? How would you say these words?

1. **aisling** – dream
   a) /ash-ling/
   b) /aysh-ling/

2. **teach** – house
   a) /teetch/
   b) /chokk/

3. **leabhar** – book
   a) /lee-ber/
   b) /lyau-wer/
   c) /lyaw-ver/

4. **múinteoir** – teacher
   a) /mayn-tor/
   b) /mooin-tchore/
   c) /mooin-tcheer/

5. **máthair** – mother
   a) /mawth-er/
   b) /maw-her/

6. **mac** – son
   a) /mok/
   b) /mek/
   c) /muk/

7. **tuar ceatha** – rainbow (prophecy of a shower!)
   a) /tur katha/
   b) /toowar kahha/

8. **spéaclaí** – glasses (spectacles)
   a) /spay-ak-lee/
   b) /spek-lee/

You'll find the **freagraí** – answers to this exercise at the end of the book.

5

Conas Atá Muid?
How Are We?

When you learn that Irish pronunciation is highly consistent, you begin to click with the language. Every time you practice, you are stoking the fire. Basically, when we release ourselves from our **Béarla** – English-centric mindset, we come to terms with Irish being a different language. And, actually, one which makes a lot of sense.

English has around 8 sounds indicated by the letter 'c'. It can sound like /k/ /s/ /ks/ /tʃ/ /ʃ/ /q/ or even be silent: cold, city, eccentric, cello, ancient, cucumber and muscle. If we think of the 'Pacific Ocean', 'c' appears three times and makes three different sounds.

In contrast, 'c' in Irish has one sound when followed by any letter other than 'h'. For example, the question words in Irish start with a hard /k/ sound.

Conas – How?

The letter 'o' sounds like /uh/, as in 'bull'. The letter 'a' sounds like the vowel sound /ɒ/ in 'clock', and the stress is on the first syllable, so the last syllable is unstressed. **Conas** sounds like /KUN-uss/.

When there is a **fada,** an accent over the vowel, it is stressed: **Conas atá tú?** /KUN-uss at-AW TOO/ – How are you?

As I mentioned in the previous chapter, I believe the use of phonemes is slightly restrictive. Pronunciation is much more than saying something correctly; it's about rhythm, intonation and emotion.

When we say **Fáilte** – Welcome, we are not saying /FAWL–cha/ which is flat and might be interpreted in different ways by different readers, depending on first-language interference or accent. We hear the long **á** sound, we smile into the 'i', (into the eyes, says you!) and then comes the slender 't' /tch/ and the schwa sound of the final **e**, a lazy vowel sound. What we say sounds more like a sped up /FAW-il-tcheh/.

Say it out loud. Get your tongue around those sounds. Start to see **Conas atá tú?** and hear it without smothering it in English vowels and affectations. Learning the pronunciation is key to appreciating the intricate and intelligent language system. Of course, our mouths are used to making certain sounds and it takes time to practice new ones, but it is brilliant for the **inchinn** – brain and the **béal** – mouth, to have a go. Learning a line for a wedding or something to shout onstage if you're touring and happen to be in Ireland is all well and good, but if you are here to connect with the language, I would highly recommend taking the relatively short amount of time to learn the sounds. Use what you're learning and stretch and challenge yourself to remember it, too.

Usage and recall are the two pillars of language acquisition. Feel the words fill up your mouth. Hear them in your voice. Write down what you're learning. See them in your handwriting. Charge the air around you with them.

It's common in Ireland to ask, 'How are ye?' And for the response to be 'How are ye? **Aon scéal?**' – Any story? It doesn't mean 'Tell me a story', but simply, how's it going? I think the Irish knack for storytelling was honed over many generations of fireside gatherings fuelled by **poitín** – poteen, but also due to the structure of our native language. According to Matthew S. Dryer's 2013 study in the *World*

Atlas of Language Structures, only 6.7% of all the world languages start sentences with the verb, and this brings a sense of urgency, action and immediacy to the forefront.

In fact, **scéal** – story – comes from Proto-Indo-European **sek^w* ('to say'), so this verb-subject-object structure means that we don't simply say something in Irish, we tell a story. We have a **seanfhocal** – proverb: **An té a bhíonn siúlach bíonn scéalach**, meaning 'The one who is a walker is a talker', or the one who walks has stories to tell, and the Irish are well-known for travelling far and wide. To quote Maeve Binchy, one of Ireland's most esteemed writers, 'In Ireland, every place you visit and every person you meet has a story. And they love to tell you their stories. Everyone is interested in everything; in a land of storytellers, you will never be bored'.

Other languages which use this Verb-Subject-Object structure include Arabic, Classic Maya, Tagalog, Tongan and Hawaiian. A shared feature of these languages is that they lack the verb 'to have'. They employ locative structures ('at me exists'), existential phrases ('there is'), or relational nouns ('mine') to convey ownership. In Irish, the object is 'at me'. A student of mine, a Hungarian lawyer, once said to me, 'There is a big difference between ownership and possession, and Irish appears to eschew both!'

In starting the sentence with the verb, we hear echoes of how we speak English in Ireland – Hiberno-English, or English from Hibernia, the land of winter. Says she to me! And says I to her! We speak English using Irish words, phrases and structures. **Deir sí liom** – says she to me. And we have preserved our native, indigenous language, our thoughts, our tenderness, our humour and our wisdom. A friend of mine, the talented storyteller, performer and actor Órla McGovern talks about how the syntax (or structure) of Irish sentences holds a quintessential consciousness of the space. In a story about a stolen bicycle: There it was, up against the wall – gone!

This is how we are. How are you? **Conas atá tú?** We have four main ways of saying 'How are you?' in Irish, depending on where we're from:

- **Cén chaoi a bhfuil tú?** – What way are you in? In the west in Connacht.
- **Cad é mar atá tú?** – What is it as you are? In the north in Ulster.
- **Conas atá tú?** – How are you? In the east in Leinster, and in the Official Standard.
- **Conas tánn tú?; Conas taoi?** – How are you? In the south in Munster.

I like to use all of them, almost as if I am honouring the places I learned them or heard them, and my teachers and family who use them. We can be struck by cynics who say 'We don't say it like that here' but language is about communicating, and being understood; it's fluid and accommodating, not restrictive. Often the wisest and most expansive ideas come from experience, knowing that the less rigid you are the more you can play with freedom, and explore. This goes for pronunciation, too. The more confident you become that making mistakes, being playful and trying things out for the sake of it is not a promotion of ignorance, but a linguistic celebration.

CLEACHTADH – PRACTICE

Let's have a **comhrá beag** – little conversation: **Mise agus tusa** – me and you.

> **Mise: Conas atá tú?** /KUN-iss at-AW TOO/ – How are you?

> **Tusa: Tá mé go maith agus tusa?** /taw may guh mah – OGG-iss TUSS-sa/ – I am well, and you?

> **Mise: Tá mé go hiontach** /taw may guh HEEN-tokk/ – I am great.

6

Níl Focal ar (?) agus (?)
No Word for Yes or No

Have you ever heard a conversation between Irish people which goes something like:

'Are you Mollie?'
'I am.'
'Do you live in Dublin?'
'I do.'
'Have you got a brother?'
'I have!'
'Would you like a cup of tea?'
'I wouldn't now, I've had a few.'

We tend to avoid saying Yes and No in Hiberno-English. This is because there are no words for Yes or No **as Gaeilge**; no umbrella term for affirming or negating. We answer the question with the verb. Take **snámh** – 'to swim':

- **An snámhann tú?** – Do you swim?
- **Snámhann mé** – I swim
- **Ní shnámhann mé** – I don't swim.

This helps us process language on a much deeper level. If, in English, someone is blathering on and you're not really listening, you can get away with pretending to listen.

'Ah yeah … I think so, yeah …' with no idea what they just said! But in Irish, we must listen for the verb in question. Remember, the verb comes at the beginning of the sentence, so its prominence is helpful in navigating the response.

Not having a word for 'yes' or 'no' comes with its challenges. One might think that it prevents you from lying, since you must utter a statement according, and directly related, to the question. Is there a formality to it? There is a consciousness, an intimacy, an honesty to replying in kind. It fosters connection and oneness – the speakers feel there is a degree of listening, understanding and responsiveness.

A student of mine told me that he grew up with an Irish father who insisted on a full answer, including the verb, or at least a recognition of the verb. He wouldn't take yes or no for an answer! He would ask:

'Son, will you mow the lawn?'
'Yeah'
'You will?'
'Yes, dad.'
'Will you mow it or not?'
'I will!'

'The inward yes' – the pulmonic ingressive, is another example of closeness and accordance to a shared understanding. Older Irish people tend to use this breathy, almost laugh-like way of responding positively. This is simply breathing in while speaking, instead of breathing out, usually while saying, 'yeah, yeah'. It also exists in Scandinavian countries and sounds exactly the same. It seems to have emigrated from Ireland during the Famine to Canada. One theory put forward by Robert Eklund in his 2008 study, 'Pulmonic ingressive phonation: Diachronic and synchronic characteristics, distribution and function in animal and human sound production and in human speech', is that the Vikings brought the pulmonic ingressive to the Celts who, in turn, brought it to Atlantic Canada. The use of the pulmonic ingressive as an inward yes can be seen as a way of agreeing, or establishing closeness.

Déan, Feic, Bí – Do, See, Be

Another way we respond in kind, which English has adopted from our Celtic languages, is the 'do support'. The auxiliary in English, the helping verb 'to do' is used with most active verbs: Do you agree? I do.

In Irish, the verb **Déan** – to do/make isn't a helping verb in the same way. We don't need it. We say:

- **An aontaíonn tú liom?** – Agrees you with me?
- **Aontaíonn mé leat** – I agree with you.
- **Ní aontaíonn mé leat** – I don't agree with you.

In so many cases of English-centric thought, or 'dominant language presupposition', we try to impose English on another language. In this case, it was actually the Celtic languages which introduced the idea of the auxiliary verb, the 'do' support.

Do you take this person to be your lawfully wedded … ? I do. This 'do' is thanks to our Celtic language.

Other languages like Spanish and Portuguese don't have a question particle, a word signifying that it's a question.

¿Hablas español? You speak Spanish? *Falas português?* You speak Portuguese? They just have a punctuating question mark, or two!

In Irish, we have question particle words: **Ar** for the past, and **An** for the Present and Future. It turns into 'do' in English, how 'do' supports the other verb. Learners of Irish feel compelled to use this verb 'do' – they want to directly translate. This is also the case with, 'will': 'Will you see him tomorrow? I will'. In Irish, there is no equivalent word for 'will', rather it is built into the conjugated verb:

> **Feic** – to see
> **An bhfeicfidh tú amárach é?** – <u>Will you see</u> him tomorrow?
> **Feicfidh mé** – I will see.
> **Ní fheicfidh mé** - I will not see.
>
> **Déan** – 'to do/make', and **Feic** – 'to see' are both irregular verbs.

The Irish verb **Bí** (to be) is another of the 11 irregular verbs. The verb **Bí** comprises the habitual be, **Bíonn mé** (I do be) and the immediate be, **Tá mé** (I am).

The question form for this 'right now' tense is **An bhfuil?** This 'bhf' sounds like /w/ when its closest vowels are broad ('a', 'o' or 'u'). The question **An bhfuil?** /on wil/ (Is/am/are?) is always answered by **Tá** (is/am/are) or **Níl** (is not/am not/ are not). Where there is a **bhfuil**, there's a **tá**!

This verb has many uses:

- It describes: **Tá sé fuar** – It is cold (**sé** = it/he)
- It locates: **Tá sé anseo** – He is here
- It tells the time: **Tá sé a cúig a chlog** – It is five o'clock
- It shows possession: **Tá Gaeilge agam** – I have Irish (Irish is at me)
- It shows feeling: **Tá áthas orm** – I am happy (Happiness is on me)
- It depicts ongoing action: **Tá mé ag léamh** – I am (at) reading
- It depicts states of being: **Tá mé i mo mhúinteoir** – I am in my teacher (I am a teacher)

So even though when voting in a referendum, we might see **Tá** and **Níl** plastered all over the place, they don't mean 'Yes' and 'No'. They imply that the question is '**An bhfuil?**'

- **An bhfuil tú i bhfabhar?** Are you in favour?
- **Tá** – am
- **Níl** – am not

Some people think that 'Is ea' (or the shortened form "Sea') means 'Yes', and that 'Ní hea' means 'No'. However, this is not the case. They mean 'is so' and 'is not so'. These are the copula in the present tense, positive and negative, and serve to answer a classification question. For example:

- **An mála é? Is ea.** – Is it a bag? Is so/so it is.
- **An múinteoir thú? Is ea.** – Is it a teacher you are? Is so.
- **An Ceanadach thú? Ní hea.** – Is it Canadian you are? Not so.

So we can't answer any aul' verb with **is ea** and **ní hea**. That would be like saying: Do you play golf? Is so. Instead, we use the verb from the question, **An imríonn tú?** (Do you play?): **Imrím** – I play, **Ní imrím** – I don't play.

NOD IONTACH – TOP TIP

As you progress through your learning journey, try to narrate simple things to yourself during your daily actions – think, how would I say this **i nGaeilge**? It's nice to check and confirm in a dictionary like www.focloir.ie, or write it in your notebook, and completely normal to have to recheck and reconfirm! Every time you do it, you are strengthening your memory.

CLEACHTADH – PRACTICE

1. **An bhfuil sé fuar?** Is it cold?
   a) Tá.
   b) Is ea.

2. **An Éireannach í?** Is she Irish?
   a) Tá.
   b) Is ea.

3. **An bhfuil tú ceart go leor?** Are you okay?
   a) Tá.
   b) Is ea.

4. **An ealaíontóir thú?** Are you an artist?
   a) Níl.
   b) Ní hea.

5. **An leabhar maith é?** Is it a good book?
   a) Is ea.
   b) Tá.

6. **An éisteann tú le ceol?** Do you listen to music?
   a) Tá.
   b) Éistim.

7. **An bhfeicfidh mé amárach thú?** Will I see you tomorrow?
   a) Is ea.
   b) Feicfidh.

8. **An ólann tú tae?** Do you drink tea?
   a) Ní ólaim.
   b) Níl.

You'll find the **freagraí** – answers to this exercise at the end of the book.

7

Tá, Bíonn, Is
Three Ways of Being

People do be saying I do be saying 'do be', but the people who do be saying I do be saying 'do be' do be saying 'do be' themselves!

Maybe you've come across this Irishism, the habitual be – one of the ways of being. There are three distinct ways to 'be' in Irish. In English, we say: I am Mollie. I am friendly. I am at the yoga studio every morning.

In Irish, these three sentences take three different structures, because the first classifies *who* I am, the second describes *how* I am, and the third says what I generally *do be* doing.

- **Is mise Mollie** – I am Mollie.
- **Tá mé cairdiúil** – I am friendly.

- **Bíonn mé sa stiúideo ióga gach maidin** – I do be in the yoga studio every morning.

In a famous 2005 experiment, Janice Jackson at the University of Massachusetts highlighted the functionality and value of the habitual be. Studying AAE (African American English), Jackson's study shone a light on the richness and subtlety of dialect difference and how inferences are made.

Children were shown an image of Sesame Street characters Cookie Monster and Elmo. Cookie Monster is pictured laid out sick in bed, and Elmo is in the foreground, eating cookies. Cookie Monster has no cookies, he is simply **cortha cráite** – weary and anguished, in a state of repose. The children were asked, 'Who is eating cookies?' Everyone answered Elmo. When Janet asked, 'Who be eating cookies?' all the Black children answered 'Cookie Monster', while the white kids said again, 'Elmo'.

To those who use the habitual form of 'be', if you do be doing something, then you regularly or habitually do be doing it; it doesn't mean you're doing it right now. The Black children reasoned that Cookie Monster often does be eating cookies even if he isn't eating cookies *right now*. The white children questioned didn't appear to differentiate between the 'do be' and the 'is' forms.

Gaelic, Jackson noted, also uses verb forms that distinguish between habitual action and currently occurring action. The habitual be does be reminding us of the usefulness of English's many dialects.

These ways of being do be challenging to get your head around, but with patience, practice and perseverance, it clicks for the learner. Especially if I'm always hinting, 'Are you classifying or describing?' One of my catchy catchphrases! We start to distinguish between what a thing is, and how the thing is.

In English, we say, 'I am sad. I am depressed. I am anxious. I am Mollie. I am a teacher. I am here'.

In Irish, **ní hionann an mothúchán agus an duine** – the feelings do not define us. **Tá brón orm** – Sadness is on me. It is fleeting, temporary, transient. How healthy, what a relief it is, to acknowledge that our feelings come and go like clouds above us, like scattered showers and sunny spells.

In fact, in a language that has no verb 'to have' or 'to know', there is a fluidity and an understanding that the soul is immaterial. We come into life with nothing and we leave with nothing, and in a language that developed in a country that valued sharing, and at times didn't have much, how can we possess or own anything? Things are simply 'at us' or 'with us' for a while. What does this do to the way we think? Have we got an abundance mindset or a scarcity mindset because of the framing of our vocabulary? Celtic spirituality seems to be built into the language.

This is a very helpful way to think about how we feel. It invites acceptance, and awareness, and it is a robust and freeing way to release ourselves from 'owning' our feelings, relieving us of the pressure of embodying the feeling, even attachment to the feeling. **Tá brón orm** – I am sad also means 'I am sorry', and how tender is that? To recognise the sorrow that an apology warrants. This increases empathy, to be feeling sad and expressing the sorrow it has caused you to hurt someone else.

I often say to my students: If you say **brón** ten times you will burst into tears. **Brón brón brón** … no, I won't do it to you! I want you to laugh your way through this book, with some life-affirming, revelatory tears along the way, and the only loss I want you to feel, is the loss of that colonised mindset that stops you from stepping out and rooting yourself in the language of the land.

Feelings being 'upon' us might contribute to the light-heartedness and carefree essence the Irish have, that is so often depicted as 'the craic'. Despite our painful, poverty-stricken, persecuted past, the Irish are well-known for their smiling eyes and depth of expression.

With this dichotomy, straddling grief and growth, knowing they are inevitable aspects of life's journey, we learn to move more freely. We do be cold in the winter, we do be lambing in the spring, we do be lepping off the high rock into the sea in the summer, and we do be playing conkers in the autumn.

The concept of 'being' in Irish is a very specific thing. I am not simply standing, I am **i mo sheasamh** – in my standing, **i mo chodladh** – in my sleeping, **i mo shuí** – in my sitting, **i m'aonar** – on my own, **i mo luí** – in my lying down. I'm even 'in my teacher' (**i mo mhúinteoir**) when I take on a role. How we identify ourselves and how we are positioned in the world around us are marked by prepositions. Things are on me, at me, before me, behind me, beside me, above me, ahead of me, for me, to me, towards me, and within me. I believe this grants us a new lens and perspective on reality, **teanga eile** – another language, **súil eile** – another eye, which we can use to observe and act.

Labhair í agus mairfidh sí –
Speak her and she will live

Here, we introduce ourselves. Recall, and notice how the first syllable is stressed:

- **Is mise Mollie** /iss MISH-a Mollie/ – I am Mollie.
- **Agus tusa?** /OGG-is TUSS-sa/ – And you?
- **Cad is ainm duit?** /kod is ANN-um ditch/ – What is name for you?
- **Mollie is ainm dom** /Mollie iss ANN-um dum/ – Mollie is my name.

We use the idea of **féin** – self – in Irish more than English. There is a relationship between the self and the world around it which is so balanced and harmonious. It doesn't seem to make sense in other English dialects, and the writer/ podcaster Blindboy Boatclub claims that this contributes to the stale stereotype of the 'thick Paddy'. That we might say something which is seemingly redundant in other contexts: 'Ah, there you are now. It's yourself, so it is.'

- **Agus tú féin?** /OGG-iss too FAY-in/ – And yourself?
- **Nach thú féin é!** /NOKK hoo FAY-in ay/ – If it isn't yourself!

- **Is í féin atá ann!** /iss ee FAY-in at-AW onn/ – It's herself!
- **Is é féin atá ann!** /iss ay FAY-in at-AW onn/ – It's himself!

We might also pronounce the f in **féin** as a /h/ or silent sound, because this is how it's said in certain areas, and older versions spelled 'fhéin' with 'fh', which is silent.

- **Cad is ainm duit féin?** /kod iss ANN–um ditch HAY-in/ – What's your own name?

This is heard in Hiberno-English. A focus, or zoning in on another person. It highlights the presence and awareness that is closely tied to the language. Another example: Sure, maybe you're right, in your own way!

MACHNAMH – REFLECTION

A good friend once told me that teaching helps him get out of his head, and be 'in the space'. Irish, with this linguistic phenomenon of positioning feelings on us, and ourselves in relation to the world around us, helps us to appreciate our emotions, nature, relationships with others and who we are.

CLEACHTADH – PRACTICE

Fíor nó Bréagach? – True or False? Are these phrases matched correctly with their translation?

1. **féin** – self
2. **Agus tusa?** – What is your name?
3. **Cad is ainm duit?** – What is your name?
4. **Is mise** – You are
5. **i mo shuí** – in my sitting
6. **i m'Éireannach** – in my teacher
7. **bíonn** – does be

You'll find the **freagraí** – answers to this exercise at the end of the book.

8

A agus A
His and Hers

In Irish, nouns are either **firinscneach** – masculine – or **baininscneach** – feminine.

Masculine nouns generally end with the last vowel being broad (a/o/u) and feminine nouns generally end with the last vowel being slender (i/e). Think .ie (the .com for Ireland) as a way to remember the slender vowels. The English word 'broad' coincidentally has only broad vowels, and the word 'slender' has slender vowels. (We'll meet some exceptions later.)

- **Cistin** – kitchen is feminine, and typically so, since it ends on a slender vowel.
- **Seomra** – room is masculine, and typically so, since it ends on a broad vowel.

Consonants at the beginning, middle and end of words are connected by broad or slender vowels. Vowels are like the glue that sticks the words together.

Let's take the name 'Séamus' as an example. It has two syllables, two beats to the word. The central consonant 'm' is surrounded by the broad vowels 'a' and 'u'. As they are both broad vowels, they connect the syllables together and allow the central consonant to have a broad sound.

Every word (well, 99% of all the words) contains vowels and consonants that are magnetised together in this intricate and rare system, which affects not only spelling, but also pronunciation and grammar. Other languages like Turkish, Russian and Hungarian have a sort of vowel harmony, but Irish is quite unique in this aspect.

A phrase commonly memorised to drive this rule home is **'leathan le leathan, caol le caol'** – broad with broad, slender with slender.

So, words in Irish have gender: they are masculine or feminine, like in many other languages. Sometimes it seems a bit arbitrary. Why is a window feminine, but a door masculine, for example, and why does it matter? It is good to know because it aids spelling and learning mutations like the genitive case.

Ainmfhocail Bhaininscneacha – Feminine nouns

- Languages, apart from English (Béarla), and most countries. Coming from **béal** – mouth, 'Béarla' really means 'sounds'. An example of a feminine language and country is **An Fhrainicis** – French and **An Fhrainc** – France.
- Nature vocabulary: **an abhainn** – the river, **an fharraige** – the sea, **an spéir** – the sky.
- Words ending with the suffix **-lann** (roughly translating as 'place'): **an bhialann** – the restaurant (the food place), **an leabharlann** – the library (the book place), **an phictiúrlann** – the cinema (the picture place), **an ghrúdlann** – the brewery (the brewing place), **an dánlann** – the gallery (the art/craft place), **an amharclann** – the theatre (the viewing place).
- Words ending with the suffix **-óg/-eog**: **an bhróg** – the shoe, **an fhuinneog** – the window, **an tsióg** – the fairy.
- Naturally feminine words, i.e. female species of animals: **an luch** – the mouse (a male mouse is a

buck), **an bhó** – the cow, **an bhean** – the woman, **an lacha** – the duck.

- ○ Exception: **Cailín** – girl, like most nouns that end with **-ín**, is actually masculine.
- Words ending with **-(e)acht/-(a)íocht**: **an teachtaireacht** – the message, **an mhúinteoireacht** – the teaching.
- **An tír** – the land, **an teanga** – the language, **an Ghaeilge** – Irish, **Éire** – Ireland. The name **Éire** comes from a goddess, Ériu, goddess of sovereignty, fertility and the land.

Ainmfhocail Fhiriniscneacha – Masculine nouns

- Professions are masculine, despite ending with slender vowels: **an t-aisteoir** – the actor, **an búistéir** – the butcher, **an bainisteoir** – the manager, **an dlíodóir** – the lawyer, **an t-ealaíontóir** – the artist, **an múinteoir** – the teacher. These words are masculine, regardless of the gender of the person in the role.
- Words ending with **-ín/-án** are masculine, despite the slender ending on the diminutive **ín**: **an bodhrán** – the drum, **an cailín** – the girl, **an taosrán** – the pastry, **an nuachtán** – the newspaper.

When we add the definite article (**an** – the), to a masculine noun, nothing happens to the consonant-starting noun. Notice how these examples all end in a broad vowel-consonant (a, o, u):

- **bóthar** – road, **an bóthar** – the road
- **carr** – car, **an carr** – the car
- **fear** – man, **an fear** – the man

When we add the definite article (**an** – the) to a feminine noun, we add a **séimhiú** to the consonant-starting noun:

- **cathair** – city, **an chathair** – the city
- **fuinneog** – window, **an fhuinneog** – the window
- **an Ghearmáin** – (the) Germany (countries generally take an article)
- **an Danmhairg** – (the) Denmark

FÍRIC FHÁNACH – FUN FACT

If the noun is masculine, an adjective describing it is not lenited – doesn't add a **séimhiú** – **an fear mór** – the big man. If the noun is feminine, we do add a **séimhiú** to the adjective – **an bhean mhór** – the big woman. If the noun is pluralised, we also pluralise the adjective, by adding -a or

-e depending on its last vowel being broad or slender. **Na fir mhóra** – The big men (plural nouns ending on a slender consonant lenite the adjective). **Na mná móra** – The big women. Notice the article changes to **na** (the plural). Gender isn't important when we use the plural form: **na daoine** – the people, **na hainmhithe** – the animals. We add a 'h' to vowel-starting plural nouns.

The letters D, T and S don't take a **séimhiú** after 'an' because of the DNTLS rule: when any of these five letters come together – either within the word, or at the point where the two words meet – they 'block' the **séimhiú.**

If you say the sounds of these 5 letters: DNTLS /duh/, /nuh/, /tuh/, /luh/, /suh/ on repeat (give it a try!), you will hear and feel how they are being produced in the same part of the mouth. The tongue is pressing on the roof of the mouth. The lips and teeth are open. Say them quickly and repetitively: /duh/, /nuh/, /tuh/, /luh/, /suh/

If it helps you remember, think that DNTLS are like teeth: when they bash together, there is no smoothness, no **séimhiú,** and of course they sound like 'dentals'.

When a masculine noun starts with S, nothing happens to the noun following 'an':

- **siopa** – shop, **an siopa** – the shop
- **saol** – life, **an saol** – the life
- **seodra** – jewellery, **an seodra** – the jewellery

When a feminine noun starts with S, we add a 't' to the noun following 'an':

- **súil** – eye, **an tsúil** – the eye
- **sráid** – street, **an tsráid** – the street
- **an tSín** – China

When a masculine noun starts with a vowel, we add a 't-' to the noun following 'an' (think 't' for testosterone!):

- **arán** – bread, **an t-arán** – the bread
- **árasán** – apartment, **an t-árasán** – the apartment
- **am** – time, **an t-am** – the time

When a feminine noun starts with a vowel, we add nothing to the noun following 'an':

- **aimsir** – weather, **an aimsir** – the weather
- **eochair** – key, **an eochair** – the key
- **uirlis** – instrument, **an uirlis** – the instrument

While feminine nouns take a **séimhiú** after 'an' (**an bhean** – the woman), and masculine nouns don't (**an buachaill** – the boy), there are other scenarios where the opposite may feel true:

- **a bhean** – *his* woman
- **a bhuachaill** – *his* boy
- **a bean** – *her* woman
- **a buachaill** – *her* boy

The possessive 'a' (meaning 'his') has no effect on nouns beginning with vowels, while 'a' (meaning 'her') triggers the presence of 'h' before vowels:

- **a athair** – *his* father
- **a eochair** – *his* key
- **a hathair** – *her* father
- **a heochair** – *her* key

Irish keeps us on our toes! It's like we have to allow our brains to relax enough to accept that we don't get it, and switch off our overactive, questioning minds. The brain naturally works out these patterns over time, and catches up with the mind. Then they're working in unison and we realise it's clicking.

We have no indefinite article in Irish – there is no visible equivalent for the English 'a' or 'an' meaning 'one' of something.

- **Chonaic mé madra** – I saw a dog.
- **Tá rothar agam** – I have a bike.
- **Ba mhaith liom caife** – I would like a coffee.
- **Tá duine ann** – There is a person there.

This might explain why we use 'the' more in Hiberno-English, talking about 'the dinner' and 'the Christmas'. In Hiberno-English, we say things like:

- What are you up to for the Easter?
- Has he got over the Covid?
- What's the plan for the summer?
- Did you do the big shop?

CLEACHTADH – PRACTICE

Put this list of words into **dhá ghrúpa** – two groups: **baininscneach agus firinscneach** feminine and masculine.

an sliabh – the mountain
an ceann – the head
an gúna – the dress
an páipéar – the paper
an obair – the work
an lá – the day

an oíche – the night

an tseachtain – the week

an cat – the cat

an t-éan – the bird

an rud – the thing

an mhúinteoireacht – the teaching

an ghrian – the sun

an ghealach – the moon

an bricfeasta – the breakfast

an bia – the food

an chlann – the family

an t-innealtóir – the engineer

an Ghréigis – the Greek language

an lasóg – the little light

an tSeapáinis – the Japanese language

an Fhrainc – France

You'll find the **freagraí** – answers to this exercise at the end of the book.

9

Beannacht Is Ea Beannacht
A Greeting Is a Blessing

According to the Oxford English Dictionary, 'Hello' is an alteration of *hallo, hollo*, which came from Old High German '*halâ, holâ*, emphatic imperative of *halôn, holôn* to fetch, used especially in hailing a ferryman'. Another theory, also linked to nautical usage, was that it originated from *ho*, the Dutch word for 'hi'. Thomas Edison first adopted the word 'hello' as a method of initiating telephone calls. Prior to that, it was employed as an expression of surprise rather than a greeting.

Dia duit, our Irish 'Hello', is a way of blessing the person you are greeting. In fact, a blessing and a greeting in Irish are both **beannachtaí**.

Dia duit means 'God to you', or 'God for you'. **Dia** – God, **duit** – to/for you. You will hear it pronounced

/DEE-ya gwitch/ or /DEE-ya ditch/ or /JEE-ya gwit/. As with everywhere, there are different dialects, accents and regional differences. All good, as long as you're not saying 'D'ye do it?'

You might even see it written as **Dia dhuit** with a 'h'. This is a dialect variant and older version. In the Official Standard, we don't add the 'h', although we do pronounce it as if it's there. (Trust me, it gets easier from here!)

Dia duit is fierce religious, says you! While this may be the case, a lot of languages are imbued with religiosity. 'Goodbye' in English comes from 'God be with ye', but this is so normal for us to say it that we rarely even notice.

In response to **Dia duit**, we say **Dia is Muire duit** /JEE-ya is MURR-ah gwitch/ – God and Mary to you. The '**is**' here is an abbreviation of **agus** – and.

Creid é nó ná creid! – Believe it or not! My grandparents would tell me that in the past, people used to greet each other in the following manner:

- **Dia duit** – God to you
- **Dia is Muire duit** – God and Mary to you

- **Dia is Muire is Íosa duit** – God and Mary and Jesus to you
- **Dia is Muire is Íosa is Seosamh duit** – God and Mary and Jesus and Joseph to you
- **Dia is Muire is Íosa is Seosamh is Brigid duit** – God and Mary and Jesus and Joseph and Brigid to you
- **Dia is Muire is Íosa is Seosamh is Brigid is Pádraig duit** – God and Mary and Jesus and Joseph and Brigid and Patrick to you … And all the blessed saints.

Nowadays, thankfully the top two will suffice. Let's practice:

- **Mise** – me: **Dia duit!**
- **Tusa** – you: **Dia is Muire duit!**

If we are greeting more than one person, we say **Dia daoibh** – God to you all. And responding to a hello from a group, **Dia is Muire daoibh!** – God and Mary to you all.

Although Irish is a pre-Christian language, it was heavily influenced by Christianity, since forms of writing were developed around the time Christianity arrived in Ireland. Before Christianity, the Irish likely had their own word for a deity, but *Día* became dominant due to Latin influence. The Old Irish word *déo* (plural of *día*) meant 'gods' or 'divine beings', showing it may have had pre-Christian roots.

God almighty! We do use 'God' a lot in Irish. The Irish have a distinctive way of referring to Jesus, Mary and Joseph, or God, in general – one that's more cultural than religious.

- **Le cúnamh Dé** – With the help of God (hopefully)
- **Ó mo Dhia** – Oh my God
- **Buíochas le Dia** – Thanks be to God (thankfully)

This religious influence on the Irish language extends beyond greetings. The Christian Brothers used Irish as a medium to transmit Catholic teachings, which helped reinforce religious identity through linguistic means. They were instrumental in preserving, standardising and promoting the Irish language. Their teaching methods have been criticised for being authoritarian, uncreative and prohibitively strict, and they were widely known to be active parties in abuse enacted by the Church in Ireland. They published books like Graiméar na Gaeilge – *Irish Grammar*, Graiméar Gaeilge na mBráithre Críostaí and *New Irish Grammar*, which are still widely regarded as excellent grammar texts and are still used in schools today. As cultural nationalists, their role in educating boys to be devout Roman Catholics was a key catalyst for transforming the literacy levels and stigma of the impoverished underclass.

Of course, the control in both the classroom and the parish meant that the language adopted teachings that were aligned with religious doctrine, and began shaping the language with curses, blessings and ideologies of a deeply Christian worldview. Mary McAleese, our former President, said, 'We grew up in a Catholicism that was neither free nor freeing … it was a form of religious colonisation of the mind'.

Words that infer judgement are illustrative of the influence these educators and society had on vocabulary:

- **féintruailliú** (self-pollution/depravation) to mean 'masturbation'
- **coiscín** (little ban/little prevention/forbidden) for 'condom' – illegal in Ireland until 1985
- **ginmhilleadh** (abortion – coming from **gin** – birth/foetus, and **milleadh** – spoiling/poisoning)

We have access to older lexicon and lore-keepers, such as research done by Manchán Magan in his book, *Focail na mBan – Women's Words*, a gathering of Irish words for vaginas, vulvas, clitorises and periods with illustrations from 29 artists. This collection of more open-minded and beautiful expressions for the female body are radically different and wholly more positive than those previously officially accessible.

While the Catholic Church has left a deep and lasting imprint on the Irish language, shaping both its vocabulary and worldview, it was not the first force to do so. In Pre-Christian Ireland, the Irish language carried traces of a different relationship with the world: one rooted in nature, and intrinsically connected with the trees, the elements, and earth-based spirituality.

Allusions to **an saol eile** – the other world – are abundant in our folklore. The sanctity of natural sites and elemental rituals, such as the solar alignment of the Neolithic passage tomb at Newgrange, show us the connection with the land and relationship with the seasons. Portals, thin places and times of close access to the other realm are often mentioned and celebrated in our Celtic festivals of **Samhain**, **Imbolg**, **Bealtaine** and **Lúnasa**. These mark the beginning of winter, spring, summer and harvest season respectively, and merge some Christian aspects with Pagan influences.

The Ogham Tree Alphabet refers to a system where each letter of the ancient Irish Ogham script is associated with a tree or plant, drawing on the deep reverence early Irish culture had for the natural world, especially trees. It starts with the **crann beithe** – the birch tree; it is the first letter of the Ogham alphabet (⊤) and means 'the tree of life', or 'the feeding tree'. In Brehon Law, the indigenous legal system of early Ireland, destruction of a clan's sacred tree (*bile*), often an oak, was considered a grievous crime, symbolising the fall of a people's soul or sovereignty. The word 'Brehon' is derived from the Old Irish word *brithemain*, meaning judge or jurist. In Modern Irish, a judge is a **breitheamh.**

The word '**draoi**' (pronounced 'dree') is the Irish term for 'druid', a figure associated with wisdom, divination, healing and spiritual guidance, and the **dair** – oak tree. The root of 'druid' comes from Old Irish *druï, druí* ('druid; magician, wizard, diviner'), from Proto-Celtic **druwits* (literally either 'tree-knower' or 'firm knower'). It gives us the word **draíocht** – magic.

In pre-Christian Irish cosmology, as the Celts were animists, they believed that divine beings inhabited the world around them. Trees were seen as living beings, with spirits and consciousness. Druids hold ceremonies in sacred groves. Trees were a symbol of the connection between realms, with roots in the underworld, trunk in the human world, and branches reaching to the divine or sky realm. **An sceach gheal** – the hawthorn tree (bright bush) blossoms in May when we celebrate **Bealtaine** and people tie ribbons onto it and call it a 'wishing tree' or a 'fairy tree'.

Motorways have been diverted because of fairy trees. The **seanchaí** – storyteller and folklorist Eddie Lenihan campaigned for ten years against the building of the M18 motorway in Latoon, County Clare, warning people of great misfortune should they build over the 'important meeting place for supernatural forces of the region'.

These ancient beliefs still echo in the Irish we speak today, from our blessings to our **piseoga** – superstitions. Even as modern Irish evolved under colonial pressure and religious control, the deep connection to nature has endured.

(10)

Slán Gaelach
An 'Irish' Goodbye

....

'**Slán**' is the Irish word for 'Goodbye' coming from the same etymological root as 'safety' and 'security'. It's where we get the expression 'so long!' In Ireland, it's common to say, 'safe home!' which comes from **slán abhaile**! Another common phrase is **slán go fóill** – bye for now! To other English speakers, this phrase might seem strangely ominous, as if we're wishing someone safety *for now*, but it's really just another example of how language reflects culture.

The 'Irish Goodbye', confusingly, is slang for a kind of quick exit one makes without saying goodbye. Sneaking out during a party, hoping people won't notice your absence. Wanting to avoid the long–winded handshaking, launching into new stories, or having another drink pressed into your hand. Any Irish person will tell you it's a misnomer, since the Irish take a long time to say goodbye, and even if saying 'bye' over the phone, it'll be 'bye bye bye b–bye, b–bye, bye now, God bless, Take care now, Look after yourself, On you go. I'll let you go. Off you go. Alright. B–bye. Byyyyyyyyye b–b–b–b–b–b–b–b–bye.' This can be done with extra dramatic effect by holding the phone close to your mouth and then slowly drawing it further away as if you're physically retreating from the other person before hanging up.

There are accounts of Irish people not trusting the house phone when it was introduced to Ireland, and thinking they needed to speak louder to be heard better if the caller was in the United States, and quieter if the person was only over in Liverpool.

Speaking of Liverpool, because so many Irish people emigrated to the towns and cities of northern England, like Manchester and Liverpool, the expression 'Ta-ra!' became commonplace. It's said to derive from **Tabhair aire** – take care. According to the Oxford English Dictionary, 'ta-ra' is a playful, nursery-style version of goodbye first recorded in 1837. Tony Birtill's great book *A Hidden History: An Ghaeilge i Learpholl – The Irish Language in Liverpool*, mentions an old-fashioned Liverpool slang phrase 'Ter rar wak', meaning 'Goodbye, son', which literally comes from the expression **Tabhair aire, a mhac** /toor arreh, ah wok/ – **Take care, son.**

Irish colloquialisms or 'Irish slang' you might see in an article entitled 'Top Irish phrases to learn for your trip to the Emerald Isle' tend to be solely in English – things like 'banjaxed', 'sound', and 'grand'. The list might be interpreted as the way the Irish speak but it refers to how Irish people speak English, not how they express something in the Irish language. A confusion arises. **Mearbhall** is confusion, coming from Old Irish: *merfall* (a crazy turn). I marvel at this word, and how other confusions arise from our way of speech. Confusion is healthy and welcome in learning. If you're not confused, you're not concentrating! Even the simplest things to say in Irish take a deep level of understanding. Trying to hold on too tightly to rules and remember the **séimhiú** here and the **urú** there, and also not having fully grasped a concept, is completely normal. We realise that when we let loose a little, and accept that we don't know, and that's ok, we start to make progress. **Foighne, cleachtadh, dianseasmhacht** – patience, practice, perseverance.

FÍRIC FHÁNACH – FUN FACT

Different words are used to express an affirmative 'cool' around Ireland, in Irish, used as a common response to an idea or a plan. You might hear **Foirfe** (perfect) in Leinster and Munster, **Togha** (grand/cool) in Connacht and **Ar dóigh** (great) in Ulster.

CLEACHTADH - PRACTICE

Seo dúshlán duit – Here is a challenge for you. Habits are reflections of our choices. They take time to build and strengthen. What shines is what is important to us. Get into the habit of saying **Slán** – 'Goodbye' at the shop, or **Tabhair aire** – 'Take care' when you hang up the phone. Palms are sweaty, knees weak, arms are heavy … I get it! But this is how we start practising an exercise of integrity. **Éireoidh sé níos éasca!** – It will get easier! You can start with 'So long' or 'Ta ra' and gradually start to incorporate the Irish words. The results will surprise you. A lot of my students report that once they start, they notice Irish speakers coming out of all the corners! When people say, 'No one speaks Irish', it's because no one is speaking with them. They don't hear it because they don't invite it, or the people who speak Irish don't know that they speak Irish too. **Bain triail as!** – Give it a go!

11

Ó Shean go Nua
From Old to New

Times have changed and now we have less intricate and lengthy greeting systems, and so how we send correspondence has changed. Gone are the long form and the formal, especially in chat messages. Thankfully the art of writing letters is not dead. Lots of my students have met a **cara pinn** – pen friend in our community and they write **cártaí poist** – postcards and **litreacha** – letters in Irish to each other.

Did you know that writing helps your speaking skills? There is a well-established understanding in neuroscience which shows that one area of the brain (Broca's area) is mostly responsible for output (speaking and writing) and another part of the brain (Wernicke's area) is mostly responsible for input (listening and reading), as outlined in 'Broca–Wernicke Theories: A historical perspective' in

Handbook of Clinical Neurology (2022). This means that even if we are not speaking regularly, or immersed in a community of speakers, we can still be practising output. When we are consciously forming sentences and thinking about structure, that practice is strengthening our output skills, including our speech. **Dea-scéala** – Good news! Since we have ample access to chat groups and online forums, why not practice by scribbling something there? If you're afraid of making a mistake, remember – **is as na botúin a fhoghlaimíonn muid** – it is from the mistakes that we learn. As we become comfortable in trying and correcting, we cultivate a new mindset of growth and accuracy. And the more often you write your **dialann bhuíochais** – gratitude diary **nó liosta siopadóireachta** – or shopping list in Irish, the more you will feel that the language is singing in your bones, and is more readily accessible to you.

A nice way to start a letter could be **Is fada an lá ó chuala mé uait** – It's long the day since I heard from you. We sign off an email or a letter with **Beir bua!** – Grab victory! Or **Meas mór** – Big respect. Both are very powerful, and in absolute contrast to the stale and formal 'Best wishes/Kind regards'.

My grandmother's **grá mór** could also work, depending on the recipient. Love in Irish is not as mortifying as in English, so even if a student wishes me **grá mór**, I don't assume, 'They are in love with me!' I see it as a nourishing, universal love for all beings. It feels both bigger and less daunting than 'love'. The word and concept shift in Irish. A different consciousness emerges and layers of not only symbolism but action, take over. Since it was the last thing my grandmother would say to end a phone call, or after a chat, it was likely the last thing I ever heard her say. That is quite emotional to think about, especially since I have students on the other side of the world who learn this phrase to greet their baby grandchildren for the first time. That being said, maybe don't use 'grá mór' at the end of a work email.

Go dtí an chéad uair eile – Until next time, is also appropriate. To finish my emails, I use **le gach dea-ghuí** – with every good wish.

If we are abbreviating in texts or in online conversations, it is common to use these short forms:

GRMA (Go raibh maith agat) – Thank you

Míle b! (Míle buíochas) – A thousand thanks

LDT (Le do thoil) – Please (to one person)

LBT (Le bhur dtoil) – Please (to multiple people)

TFR (Tá fáilte romhat) – You're welcome

SGF (Slán go fóill) – Bye for now

GOA (Gáire os ard) – Laughing out loud

BLD (Buíochas le Dia) – Thanks be to God/Thankfully

NASAA (Níl ach saol amháin agat) – YOLO! You only live once

OMD (Ó mo Dhia) – OMG – Oh my God

CGL (Ceart go leor) – Ok/alright

FAB (Fadhb ar bith) – No problem at all (not 'Fab!' for Fabulous!)

TBO (Tá brón orm) – I'm sorry

NBB (Ná bí buartha) – Don't worry

DS (Deireadh seachtaine) – Weekend

BB7B (Beir bua agus beannacht) – All the best wishes (literally, 'grab victory and blessing!')

Srl. (agus araile) – and so on, etc.

Some slang includes:

- **Brónsies** is a short/cute way of saying **Tá brón orm** – I'm sorry, maybe for when you're sorry, not sorry …
- 'Sounds like a prob **leat** rather than a prob **liom**' – This is used for those situations when it's someone else's problem and not yours (**leat** – with you, **liom** – with me)

CLEACHTADH – PRACTICE

Since we are often employing the same expressions online, repeating things, reacting to things with a thumbs up, or praise, or exclamations, let's look at some common and useful comments and phrases to post to show your excitement, joy, encouragement and empathy.

Match the situation with the appropriate reaction. They are all jumbled up.

If they're all new to you, see where your intuition takes you. If they're familiar, take a moment to stretch your memory (answers at the back of the book!):

Someone announces their good news	**Tá tú go hálainn**
Someone has a baby	**Tá cuma bhlasta air!**
Someone is looking great	**Comhghairdeas**
You want to support a sports team	**Slán turais**
Someone is nervous because they have an exam	**Lá Breithe Sona duit!**
Someone is off on a trip	**Fáilte chuig an domhan**
Someone posts about losing a loved one	**Corcaigh abú! Maigh Eo abú! Éire abú!**
Someone is making a delicious dish	**Sláinte!**
Someone is celebrating their birthday	**Ádh mór**
Someone is celebrating with a toast	**Mo chomhbhrón**

Well, how did you get on? Remember, it's only **scanrúil** – scary the first few times. And vulnerability attracts openness, respect and connection. Also, you will be teaching others by posting in Irish. I like to post bilingually to be more accessible and inclusive. **An tslí is fearr chun foghlaim ná múineadh!** – The best way to learn is to teach!

(12)

Más É Do Thoil É
If It Is Your Will

I never really thought saying 'please' could come across as impolite or abrasive, but in comparison to its Irish equivalent, it can sound surprisingly demanding.

In English, the word 'please' comes from 'if it pleases you' from the Old French word *plaisir* (meaning 'to please' or 'to give pleasure'), which itself comes from the Latin *placere* ('to be agreeable' or 'to satisfy'). However, in the 17th century, it was shortened to 'please', and became a polite request, rather than a full phrase. Nowadays, it is a common courtesy word used to soften commands. Likewise, the French use *s'il vous plaît*, and the Spanish *por favor*. They all slightly vary in meaning from the Irish **más é do thoil é** – if it is your will/your wish or **le do thoil** with your will/your wish. The Irish phrasing subtly grants the listener agency, and adds an element of a boundaried request. To order a

pionta Guinness, le do thoil – pint of Guinness, with your will, allows for a sense of collaboration. This etiquette is highly prevalent in Ireland, with usage of polite, softening words like please, thank you, you're welcome, sorry, and excuse me being far more frequent than our neighbouring countries.

When I lived in Spain I found it hard to order something so directly – *Me-da un café* – Give me a coffee, or *Ponme un café* – Put me a coffee. It felt rude. In Dublin, I was used to a nauseating level of obsequiousness and politeness when ordering something in English that is not conducive to honesty or connection – 'Sorry! If you don't mind, when you get a chance, would it be ok to have a coffee, please? Thank you so much. Cheers. Thanks! Thanks a mil. Sorry.'

In Irish, conversely, we say things directly – **Ba mhaith liom caife** – I would like a coffee, literally 'would be good with me a coffee'. Of course, we add in a 'please' – **le do thoil** – with your wish or **más é do thoil é** – if it is your wish.

How tender and thoughtful, to include and consider the will of the other person who may accede to your demand. It heightens empathy. It is not just you asking for something pleasantly – that would be transactional. It is relational. I like how the Irish 'le do thoil' retains its full complexity of connection between what I would like and what would please you to give me. There is mutual gratification involved.

When ordering in Irish, an excellent way to increase your usage of the language and bring it into the wild, use this structure:

Ba mhaith liom meaning literally: would be good with me. Instead of liking something, we say **Is maith liom** – Is good with me (I like). So in the conditional, this becomes: **Ba mhaith liom** – I would like.

Ba mhaith liom cupán tae, le do thoil – I would like a cup of tea, please. Associating the /w/ sound at the beginning of **mhaith** and the /l/ sound at the start of **liom**, we might connect the two: I would like – **Ba mhaith liom.**

The **séimhiú** (smoothening), lenition (adding a 'h' after a consonant) comes in there since it's easier to say **Ba mhaith** /buh wah/ than **Ba maith** /buh mah/. In the latter, you need to close your lips twice. In the former, feel one smooth transition from one to the other. We add a **séimhiú** in the conditional copula structure.

In English, 'thank you', comes from Middle English *thanken*, from Old English *þancian, þoncian* 'give thanks; to recompense, to reward', from Proto-Germanic **thankōjanan* (source also of Old Saxon *thancon*, Old Norse *þakka*, Danish *takke*, Old Frisian *thankia*, Old High German *danchon*, Middle Dutch/Dutch/German *danken* 'to thank'), from **thankoz* 'thought; gratitude' (from PIE root **tong* – 'to think, feel'). It is related to the Old English *þanc, þonc*, originally 'thought', but also 'good thoughts, gratitude'. It stems from 'I think of what you did for me'.

In Irish, we say **Go raibh maith agat** – May you have goodness. Since Irish has no direct verb for 'to have', we use the preposition **agat** – at you, with the subjunctive form **Go raibh** – May it be or that it were.

We can add emphasis by adding **míle** – a thousand – as in **Go raibh míle maith agat** – May you have a thousand goodnesses. Feel free to add as many **míle** as you like, there's no limit to gratitude in Irish – **Go raibh míle míle míle míle maith agat** – a trillion thanks!

This subjunctive form is also used for blessings and curses. We hear it in the Lord's Prayer: **Go dtaga do ríocht** – may your kingdom come, or in hilarious Irish insults –

Go n-ithe an cat thú agus go n-ithe an diabhal an cat –
May the cat eat you and may the devil eat the cat. We use it
to wish someone good luck: **Go n-éirí an bóthar leat** – May
the road rise with you, and to give a toast or a blessing: **Go
maire tú an céad** – May you live to be a hundred!

Thank you is such a short phrase to convey something as
deep and layered as **Go raibh maith agat.** There we have
maith again, and in Irish, it could appear multiple times in
one short conversation.

Imagine a coffee shop scenario:

A. '**Maidin mhaith!** – Good morning!'
B. '**Maidin mhaith!** – Good morning!'
A. '**Conas atá tú?** – How are you?'
B. '**Tá mé go maith!** – I'm good.'
A. '**Maith thú!** – Well done!'
B. '**Maith an fear!** – Good man!'
A. '**Ba mhaith liom caife, le do thoil.** – I would like a
    coffee, please.'
B. '**An-mhaith. Ar mhaith leat bainne?** – Very good.
    Would you like milk?'
A: '**Ba mhaith.** – I would like.' '**Go raibh maith agat** –
    Thank you'

B. 'Bíodh lá <u>maith</u> agat – Have a good day'
A. '<u>Maith</u> dom – Forgive me. **Siúcra, chomh <u>maith</u>.** – Sugar, as well.'
B. '<u>Maith</u> go leor – All good.'

Go leor is where we get 'galore' from, meaning, 'in abundance'. Already, we've seen examples galore of the word '**maith**'.

Well, if that wasn't a smashing conversation altogether! Smashing, meaning 'brilliant' comes from **is maith sin** – that's good. Many people believe the name of Chicago rock band The Smashing Pumpkins comes from the physical smashing of pumpkins, but the band got in touch with me to say it really derives from 'smashing' in an Irish sense, **is maith sin.**

Another derivation of '**maith**' is the Dublin slang 'moth'. When I was a teenager, it was common for a boy to call a girl his 'moth' (pronounced /mot/) if they were dating, and apparently it means 'my good thing, my goodness'.

To express 'you're welcome', we'll use **fáilte** (welcome) and in true Irish style, emphasise it as much as possible. Irish being so emphatic, so over the top, we'll add not one, not two, but one hundred thousand welcomes. Or sometimes just twenty-one of them.

- **Céad míle fáilte** – 100,000 welcomes
- **Fáilte is fiche** – A welcome and 20

We can also position the welcome: **Tá fáilte romhat** – There is welcome before you. I think of a red carpet being laid out in someone's honour. There is welcome before you – come on in, come here to me.

CLEACHTADH – PRACTICE

Coffee shops, bars, restaurants, cafés and ice-cream parlours around Ireland sometimes offer discounts to those who order **as Gaeilge**.

Here are some useful phrases, which might get you a euro off your next pint! Since 'mhaith' is the most important word here, we will stress it slightly.

- **Cad ba mhaith leat?** /kod buh WAH lat/ – What would you like?
- **Ba mhaith liom** /buh WAH lum/ – I would like
- **Pionta Guinness** /PYUN-ta Guinness/ – a pint of Guinness

- **Pionta beorach** /PYUN-ta BYOR-okk/ – a pint of beer
- **Gloine fíona** /GLIN-yeh FEE-yun–ah/ – a glass of wine
- **Gloine uisce** /GLIN-yeh ISH-keh/ – a glass of water
- **Cupán tae** /kupp-awn tay/ – a cup of tea
- **Cupán caife** /kupp-awn KAFF–eh/ – a cup of coffee
- **Uisce beatha** /ISH-keh BAH-hah/ – a whiskey (water of life!)
- **Canna cóic** /KON-na koh-ik/ – a can of coke
- **Sú oráiste** /soo ur-AWSH-ta/ – orange juice

Remember, we have no indefinite article, the formal term for 'a' in Irish.

- **Le do thoil** /leh duh hul/ – Please (with your will/wish)
- **Más é do thoil é** /mawsh ay duh hul ay/ – Please (if it is your will/wish)
- **Go raibh maith agat** /GUH rev MAH og-gut/ – Thank you.
- **Tá fáilte romhat** /taw FAW-il-tcheh ROH-wat/ – You're welcome.

Bertie Ahern Fianna Fáil TD

....

The Irish language only has eleven irregular verbs. English has 220. Other languages have up to 600! In Irish, of these eleven, only six are what I term 'super irregular'. The rest are somewhat straightforward.

As you'll see, these are the most useful and common verbs in any language: **to be, to say, to see, to get, to go, to do, to hear, to give, to eat, to come, to grab.** One of them, somewhat mysteriously **Beir** – to grab/to bear, is not that common, but might hint at what was common usage in bygone times, in older versions of the language. And I suppose, it's where we get the verb 'to be born':

- **Rugadh mé i mBaile Átha Cliath** – I was born in Dublin.
- **Cár rugadh thú?** – Where were you born?

How am I going to remember these, **a deir tú** – says you? Here is a handy **acrainm** – acronym for the six super irregulars:

Bertie Ahern Fianna Fáil TD

- **Bí** – to be
- **Abair** – to say
- **Feic** – to see
- **Faigh** – to get
- **Téigh** – to go
- **Déan** – to do/make

Bertie Ahern was our **Taoiseach** (Chief, or Prime Minister) when I was a **cailín óg** (a young girl) and he was a member of Fianna Fáil. Fianna Fáil is a political party in Ireland, which means 'Soldiers of Destiny'. He was a **teachta dála** – a member of parliament, known as a 'TD'.

If Bertie Ahern and Fianna Fáil are not familiar to you, you could learn Bring All French Fries To Dinner!

These six verbs are the super irregulars. They break some rules, they dabble with confusion. But **buíochas le Dia** – thanks be to God, there's only six of them! This is to say, regular verbs, the other hundreds of verbs, are incredibly patterned and consistent, and easy to conjugate.

The other five irregulars are not that irregular. These are:

- **Clois** – to hear
- **Beir** – to grab/bear
- **Tabhair** – to give
- **Ith** – to eat
- **Tar** – to come

You could remember them by this mnemonic: Cute Bear tis Irish terrain – **Clois Beir Tabhair Ith Tar.** Ireland looks like a cute bear. The outline of the island resembles a teddy bear waiting for a hug.

Go bunúsach – basically, a regular verb follows a very easy pattern. For example, to put regular verbs in the **aimsir chaite** – past tense, we conjugate them by simply adding a **séimhiú** (h). Think 'h' for history!

A handy rhyme to remember this:

Roses are red
Violets are blue

Every regular verb in the Past Tense
Takes a ... **séimhiú**!

The **séimhiú** – softening comes in as the second letter.
For example:

- **Bris** – to break, becomes **bhris** – broke
- **Glan** – to clean, becomes **ghlan** – cleaned
- **Ceannaigh** – to buy, becomes **cheannaigh** – bought

Verbs like **ól** – to drink and **fan** – to wait/stay are in a special
category of verbs beginning with a vowel or with the letter
'f' (which sounds silent when it has a **séimhiú**). These take
a D' in the positive form:

Ól – to drink
D'ól mé – I drank.
Níor ól mé – I didn't drink.
Ar ól tú? – Did you drink?

Fan – to wait/stay
D'fhan mé – I waited/
stayed.
Níor fhan mé – I didn't
wait/stay.
Ar fhan tú? – Did you wait/
stay?

Remember L, N, R don't take a **séimhiú**:

- **Léigh** – to read
- **Léigh mé an nuachtán inné** – I read the newspaper yesterday
- **Nigh mé** – I washed
- **Rith mé** – I ran

These 11 irregulars, however, change their form quite a bit when they conjugate.

They're not just adding a **séimhiú**. Here is a **scéal** – story to learn and remember them:

Bí – to be, **Bhí** – was	**Bhí mé sa pháirc** – I was at the park
Abair – to say, **Dúirt** – said	**Dúirt mé, 'Dia duit' le gach duine** – I said 'Hello' to everyone
Feic – to see, **Chonaic** – saw	**Chonaic mé madra álainn** – I saw a beautiful dog
Faigh – to get, **Fuair** – got	**Fuair mé mo pheann** – I got/found my pen

Téigh – to go, **Chuaigh** – went	**Chuaigh mé thall** – I went over
Déan – to do, **Rinne** – did	**Rinne mé líníocht** – I did/ made a drawing
Tabhair – to give, **Thug** – gave	**Thug mé don úinéir í** – I gave it to the owner
Tar – to come, **Tháinig** – came	**Tháinig mé abhaile** – I came home
Clois – to hear, **Chuala** – heard	**Chuala mé an bháisteach** – I heard the rain
Ith – to eat, **D'ith** – ate	**D'ith mé mo lón** – I ate my lunch
Beir – to grab/to bear **Rug** – grabbed	**Rug mé barróg ar mo chat** – I grabbed a hug on my cat

In the **Aimsir Láithreach** – Present tense, **Aimsir Fháistineach** – Future tense, **Modh Coinníollach** – Conditional mood, and other structures, the irregular verbs follow a pattern that is closer to the regular verbs, for example:

- **Bí** – to be, **Bíonn** – does be, **Beidh** – will be
- **Feic** – to see, **Feiceann** – sees, **Feicfidh** – will see

- **Déan** – to do/make, **Déanann** – does/makes, **Déanfaidh** – will do/will make
- **Clois** – to hear, **Cloiseann** – hears, **Cloisfidh** – will hear
- **Beir** – to grab, **Beireann** – grabs, **Béarfaidh** – will grab

Ith – to eat is maybe the most normal of all the irregular verbs. It acts completely normal in the past, adding a D' like all the regular verbs. It shows no sign of strangeness in the present, adding an '-eann' ending like the other slender short verbs. But in the future tense, we see how **Ith** is not as **íosfaidh** as it seems!

- **D'ith mé** – I ate
- **Itheann mé** – I eat
- **Íosfaidh** – will eat, sounds like 'easy'

NOD IONTACH – TOP TIP

I would recommend associating auditory or visual triggers to these irregular verbs, to help them stick in your memory. Things like **thug** (gave) sounds like 'hug', and we 'give hugs', or **bhí** (was) sounds like 'V' – think V for Vintage, since it's the **Bí** verb in the past. There is a hilarious meme of Leonardo DiCaprio eating **ceapairí** – sandwiches, and in Irish it says: **Cad a d'ith Leo?** What did Leo eat? **Leonardo d'ith ceapairí-o!**

CLEACHTADH – PRACTICE

How would you put these verbs into the past tense?

> **Dún** – to close
> **Cuir** – to put
> **Múin** – to teach
> **Rith** – to run
> **Nigh** – to wash
> **Siúil** – to walk
> **Ceap** – to think
> **Labhair** – to speak
> **Éirigh** – to get up/rise
> **Foghlaim** – to learn
> **Mínigh** – to explain

You'll find the **freagraí** – answers to this exercise at the end of the book.

(14)

Sanasaíocht Sanasaíochta
The Etymology of Etymology

The **sanasaíocht** – etymology, offers us the story of the word. This is what has defined my teaching. If we are to learn a word in isolation, there is little chance we will remember it. It is merely a cluster of sounds. However, there is magic in store if we know the reason why it sounds like that, where it came from, the meaning behind it, and how it changed over time. Fireworks go off in my brain when I trace a word back to something which makes sense, which lights up the meaning and helps me remember it since it's so vivid and alive.

The word **sanasaíocht** itself, coming from **sanas** ('gloss') + **-aíocht** (a noun suffix), enlightens us: *sanas* comes from Proto-Celtic **sanestos* ('advice; whisper'). Finding this out was a **splanc thuisceana** – lightbulb moment for me. It's one of the many juicy, invigorating feelings Irish offers when you root yourself in the language. There are words we hear or use every day in Irish without realising their full meaning. That's what ignites my passion: there is a world within the words, and the adventure of exploring it never ends. It is a constant exercise in unearthing new wonder. Here are some of my favourite discoveries:

Macalla – echo (literal meaning: son of the cliff)

Lus súgach – asparagus (literally: happy herb)

Cíoch charraige – anemone (literally: rock boob)

Madra rua – fox (literally: red dog)

Madra uisce – otter (literally: water dog)

Madra crainn – squirrel (literally: tree dog)

Madra allta – wolf (literally: wild dog). Another word for 'wolf' is **mac tíre** – son of the land, which is telling, because the grey wolf in Ireland outlasted the grey wolf in England, Scotland and Wales by about 300 years. Their existence was intrinsic to the ecosystem.

Ag bualadh craicinn – having sex (literally: banging skin)

Giorria – hare (literally: short deer from 'Gearrfhia': **Gearr** – short, **fia** – deer)

Béaloideas – folklore (literally: mouth instruction)

Staighre beo – escalator (literally: live stairs)

Talamh an Éisc – Newfoundland (literally: Land of the Fish)

Smugairle róin – jellyfish (literally: snot of a seal)

Míol mór – whale (literally: big louse)

Scréachóg reilige – barn owl (literally: graveyard screecher)

Bóín Dé – ladybird (literally: God's little cow)

Spideog – robin (**spid** – energy)

Gobadán – sandpiper (literally: little pointy beak)

Lasair choille – goldfinch (literally: bright flame of the forest)

Lus an chromchinn – flower of the bent head (daffodil)

Rí rua – red king (chaffinch)

Préachán – little perish/harbinger of death (crow)

Pocaire gaoithe – wind frolicker (kestrel)

Lus na mban sídhe – flower of the banshees (foxglove *poisonous)

Bainne bó bleachtáin – juice of the milk cow (cowslip)

Sponc – spirit/spunk/pizzazz (coltsfoot)

CLEACHTADH – PRACTICE

Can you break down these words to find smaller words hiding inside them?

grianghraf
spéirbhean
leathbhádóir
dea-scéal
nuachtlitir
seanchara
sráidbhaile
seanathair
gealgháireach

You'll find the **freagraí** – answers to this exercise at the end of the book.

Cuid a Dó
Part Two

....

Ag Cothú na Tine
Fuelling the Fire

(15)

A Bheith sa Bhaile
Belonging

Our treasured poet Seamus Heaney once said, 'Not to learn Irish [...] is to cut oneself off from ways of being at home'. In this brief sentence, he encapsulated the idea that language is not merely a tool for communication, but is fundamental to properly understand Irish identity and cultural values. Language roots us at home.

There is no verb 'to belong' in Irish. We simply say **a bheith sa bhaile** – 'to be at home'. Stories of emigrants touching down on Irish soil and feeling an ethereal sense of being home are ubiquitous. The Irish diaspora often experience a deep pull towards the language, and learning it can be both deeply cathartic and emotional. For those who grew up outside of Ireland, the language can unlock a sense of home for them. Learning the language so closely intertwined with their sense of identity and heritage allows them to feel connected to home, community, and the land. And it's not only the diaspora who can experience these feelings. Those who were raised in Ireland and learned Irish at school can also unravel the language, and root themselves in it. They can gain a greater understanding of their identity and culture, and enjoy the healing and revealing journey.

In our post-pandemic, neoliberal-leaning society, people are craving community, authenticity and a happiness that comes from self-growth and purposeful progress.

The Irish language is **fite fuaite** – interwoven, with Irish emotion. The Irish people might be seen as strong, silent types, or as masters of masking a deep intergenerational trauma and poverty with light-hearted banter. But beneath that humour, at the core of how we think, feel and laugh, is a language of deep resonant love and togetherness. When people feel that their ties to ancestry and land-based knowledge are cut off, self-harm escalates.

Being Irish means different things to different people, of course, but in an age of disharmony, distrust, discord and let's be honest, dystopian levels of destruction, the knowledge of ancestral and ancient languages is more relevant and necessary than ever. It is proven that learning a language, any language, but especially one that is significant to you in terms of ancestry, promotes feelings of comfort and freedom.

It generates a sense of oneness in society, even in disparate aspects of society. Talking to psychologist and activist Conchobhar Ruadh on the topic of decolonisation, he brings up a point about self-abuse. His studies lead him to the findings that alcoholism and substance abuse are rife in communities that have suffered through oppression and colonisation. When our land is taken from us, when we are deprived of our food sources, our dignity, and when our language is literally beaten out of us, we do what we can to survive. The self-defence mechanism of going so far as to hate ourselves, to try to be like the oppressor, is unfortunately common and part of human nature. The linguistic bomb – impactful and explosive – doesn't just eradicate language. Along with property seizure, it can remove a physical sense of home and destroy entire ways of knowing. It can sever cultures from their identity and worldview – the songs and stories and similes and syntax which envelope what is important to them and what has been handed down over generations.

Irish people have felt detached from the language for

various reasons, and this exacerbates the relationship with belonging, feeling centred and at home. In some cases, they were not given the chance to learn, as it wasn't available to them in their school or community. They might have been told that they can't learn the language, because they have dyslexia or other learning differences, further compounded by the level system – learning Irish at a lower level, or being given an exemption from learning.

Maybe they grew up outside of Ireland and felt a distance from an idea of home, or they never felt the ease of discovering their language in a non-judgemental, fun, and caring capacity. This is very common, and this is why there is a movement to **fill ar do dhúchas** – return to your origin. The word **dúchas** has four main definitions in the **foclóir** – dictionary. It can mean predisposition, origin, heritage and instinct. It is our ways, our customs, our culture. The fantastic resource **www.duchas.ie** borrows the word to share archives of stories, rhymes, hearsay and local knowledge. It is a natural affinity, a connection, with the language of the past and present.

The sense of home is redolent in how we greet each other by saying **a chara** – friend. We know this person and they are a friend. It is egalitarian and indiscriminate.

We can address even our **Uachtarán** – President with the warmth and openness of saying hello to a friend. **Uachtar** – cream, comes from the Proto-Indo-European root *h_3ewps* meaning 'high' signifying the top, or the surface. There is unity and equality built into the language. Nobody has a **lámh in uachtar** – 'a hand in cream', or the upper hand.

Indeed, President Michael D. Higgins wished us a blessed St. Patrick's Day in 2025 by saying, 'I am convinced beyond any doubt that in spite of all the challenges we face, there remains within the Irish people a profound and unyielding commitment to seeing beyond the self, to seeing the other as a friend'. Feeling at home, feeling like you belong, and feeling a sense of friendship and community is conducive to experiencing and expressing an abundance of love.

However, the fact that we are speaking a foreign language in Ireland further separates us from the land and the ancient wisdom of the place, and this has an impact on how we express ourselves. The inability or reticence to express ourselves directly might have something to do with this disconnection and the way we express love in the Irish language. In a casual survey that I conducted through Instagram, I asked my friends and followers if they felt that saying, 'I love you', was a bit cringey, a bit unnatural. They agreed. A lot of them had only recently started to express love verbally in their 30s or 40s. For them, saying **grá mór** – big love – held more meaning for them, and was easier to say, emotionally.

It could be argued that most personal and interpersonal issues come from not knowing ourselves. If someone posts a photo of themselves tanned at the beach on Instagram, or mentions their accomplishments on LinkedIn, we might say, toxically, 'He loves himself', 'Who does she think she is?', 'He's fierce fond of himself altogether!'. As Conor Creighton, the author of *The Truth about Love*, says, healing only occurs when you *do* love yourself. Learning is the same, for that matter. Creighton works with many Irish clients and he asks them outright, 'Do you love yourself?' He finds that they take this as an insult, or as a slight to say 'You act like you love yourself'. He is asking out of curiosity, to nurture a starting point of self-love. We can only do the work if we love ourselves, in a healthy, abundant, forgiving, kind and calming way.

In English, the idea of loving things is quite broad – I love this flavour of tea. I love my parents and brothers. I love a pink sky at night, shepherds' delight. In Irish, we position love as being at us – **Tá grá agam ort** – Love is at me on you. Or, **Tá grá agam duit** – Love is at me for you – I have love for you.

Here are some terms of affection to greet your loved ones when speaking to them:

- **A chuisle** – my pulse (romantic)
- **A chroí** – my heart (romantic)
- **A chuisle mo chroí** – O, pulse of my heart (romantic)
- **A mhuirnín** – my darling (romantic)
- **A rún** – my secret (romantic)
- **A stór** – my treasure (romantic)
- **A thaisce** – my precious (romantic or familiar)
- **A shearc mo chléibh** – love of my bosom … (romantic)
- **A ghrá geal** – my bright love (romantic)
- **A pheata** – my pet (familiar, for a child)
- **A leanbh** – my child/baby (familiar, for a child)
- **A mhac** – my son (familiar, for a son. Also used for 'bro'!)
- **A iníon** – my daughter (familiar, for a daughter)
- **M'úillín óir** – my little golden apple (familiar, 'my pride and joy')

Irish seems to be a more visceral, adept language at expressing closeness to another. My Nana was known for her list of abundant praise – You're a gem, what are you? You're a bundle of love. You're a dote, so you are! You're the best! What are you like? There's no one like you! Where did we get you? Floating down the Liffey on a biscuit? You're a little divileen so you are. You're a charmer!

Mol an óige agus tiocfaidh sí – Praise the youth and she will flourish

Like the customary 'Bye bye bye bye bye bye bye bye now, good luck to you, take care, God bless, chat soon, please God', of a typical Irish phone call ending, fading out as you take your mouth away from the receiver, there is an attempt, I believe to capture in English what an Irish heart wants to say. It's trying to say 'You belong. I love you.' Home is where the heart is, and at the heart of it, our Irish hearts are more at home in Irish.

All of these thoughts swirling around my head, from reading, speaking to other people in this sphere, and **ag luí isteach ar an teanga** – diving into the language, led me to writing this poem:

Irish is not an exam subject to hate
Or a diplomatic tool to placate
Or an ornamental script to put on a plate
Which we don't understand and let Google translate

Irish is our ancestral tongue
Irish is our linguistic lung
Teetering precariously low on the rung
Of endangered languages we are among

Irish is seducing learners far and wide
Those who speak freely
And those who abide
By the fascinating patterns, systems and logic
Of a language ancient enough to be our guide

Irish has been weaponised, gatekept, and punitive,
Exemptions dealt out – it's not intuitive.

I love to see Gaeilgeoirí making mistakes
It means there is effort,
We know the courage it takes

Speak with no fear
Irish is for all
Something's happening here
Answering Ireland's call.

CLEACHTADH - PRACTICE

One effective way to strengthen your vocabulary, confidence, and even writing, reading, spelling and speaking, is by keeping a daily gratitude journal. It's **sláintiúil don mheon** healthy for the mind agus **dár scileanna Gaeilge** and our Irish skills! You can use an online dictionary like **www. focloir.ie** to find new words.

Gach lá – Every day, **scríobh síos** – write down...

Trí rud a bhfuilim buíoch astu inniu – Three things I am grateful for today
> 1. **a haon** – one
> 2. **a dó** – two
> 3. **a trí** – three

They could include things like:
> **an aimsir** – the weather
> **mo chaife** – my coffee
> **barróg** – a hug
> **mo shiúl** – my walk
> **criospaí** – crisps
> **mo phost** – my job
> **mo pháirtí** – my partner

mo chlann – my family
mo chairde – my friends
mo shláinte – my health
mo pheata – my pet
ióga – yoga
mo chorp – my body
mo rothar – my bicycle
An Ghaeilge – Irish

The more you incorporate Irish into your daily practices, the more you will feel a sense of belonging, a feeling of home.

16

Domhan istigh sna Focail
A World within the Words

Feelings in Irish like **áthas** – happiness, **fearg** – anger, **sceitimíní** – excitement, **eagla** – fear are so onomatopoeic that even people who have never studied the language are able to guess what they mean – or so I've found in my casual experiments! When you hear them, you are awake to the world within the words. Adjectives like **ciúin** – quiet, **glórach** – loud, **mall** – slow and **tapa** – fast hint to the listener, and even the reader, what the word signifies. I worked at a St. Patrick's Day event once and I tried this with about 100 individuals from other countries, ranging from age 3 to 93. They managed to guess the correct word and its translation about 90% of the time.

When you take a word like **áthas** you hear the awe, you hop over the 'th', which consistently sounds like /h/ and you smile into the word. Try it out: **áthas** /AW-hiss/. That aspirated 'th' is a favourite of many students of mine. It adds levity, a bit of a bounce, to the word. When you say **Tá áthas orm** – I am happy, the muscles in the face communicate with the neurotransmitters in the brain. Like the pen in the mouth experiment, when our mouth is lifted into a smile, it tells our brain we are happy, and dopamine, serotonin and other happy hormones are released.

The feelings **fearg** – anger /FAR-ig/ and **eagla** – fear /OGG-uh-lah/ and the word **orm** – on me /URR–im/ display a signature feature of Irish, and Hiberno-English: the addition of a vowel sound between two consonants. This is called epenthesis, and we hear it in the word 'film', how Irish people can pronounce it like it has two syllables /FILL-im/. Epenthesis aids ease and flow of speech. Saying /FILL-im/ is way more craic and way easier for Irish mouths to say than /film/. Irish pronunciation, as we've seen, is all about the ease and flow of speech.

Doesn't **fearg** /FAR-ig/ sound so threatening? So pent up, so frustrated? Doesn't **eagla** /OGG-uh-lah/ sound like it's shaking with fear? Likewise, **imní** – anxiety or worry sounds like /imm-inn-ee/, some imminent danger looms.

Who knew the feelings were so cathartic in themselves? Next time you're angry, say '**Tá fearg orm**' and feel the way the plosive and forced F sound releases some pressure. A bit like saying 'Feck!' or **siúcra** – sugar when you stub your toe.

Another great example is **Tá aiféala orm** – Regret is on me. And just as freedom is always taken, never given, what goes on can be taken off.

It could be said that some of us are still dealing with crippling Irish Catholic guilt. A friend of mine studied at a Gaelscoil in Rinn, County Waterford, and she told me that instead of **brón** (sadness) being on her, she learned – **Tá cathú orm** – I'm sorry. Rather than it meaning there's sadness on me, it conveys a sense of regret. **Cathú** also means temptation. It struck me that in typical Catholic fashion, and how human psychology and even social understanding shapes language, whatever tempts you is also a regret.

Any pleasure can be a guilty pleasure if you were brought up Catholic!

NOD IONTACH – TOP TIP

We can amplify a feeling by adding on the expression: **an domhain** – of the world. So, if you are really hungry, you can say: **Tá ocras an domhain orm** – The hunger of the world is on me, or: **Tá tuirse an domhain orm** – The tiredness of the world is on me.

CLEACHTADH – PRACTICE

Even if you are totally new to Irish, see if you can guess the meaning of these words from their sound, from how they look and feel.

1. Which means 'interesting' and which means 'boring'?
   a) leadránach /lad-RAWN-okk/
   b) suimiúil /sim-yool/

2. Which means 'dry' and which means 'wet'?
   a) fliuch /flukk/
   b) tirim /TCHI-rim/

3. Which means 'fat' and which means 'thin'?
   a) ramhar /RAU-wer/
   b) tanaí /ton-nee/

4. Which means anxiety and which means peace?
   a) suaimhneas /SOO-wiv-ness/
   b) imní /im-in-ee/

5. I am happy (Happiness is on me)
   a) **Tá fearg orm**
   b) **Tá brón orm**
   c) **Tá áthas orm**

6. I am sorry
   a) **Tá cathú orm**
   b) **Tá fearg orm**
   c) **Tá sceitimíní orm**

7. **Tá aiféala orm**
   a) I am worried
   b) I regret

8. **Tá fearg orm**
   a) I am happy
   b) I am angry
   c) I am excited

9. **Tá eagla orm**
   a) I am worried
   b) I am scared
   c) I am happy

You'll find the **freagraí** – answers to this exercise at the end of the book.

17

Tá an Ghaeilge i nGach Áit
Irish Is Everywhere

Irish is listed as 'Definitely Endangered' on the UNESCO Atlas of World Languages, but the language not only survives, it flourishes, especially in the way English is spoken in Ireland and among the diaspora around the world. It's as if we're translating directly from Irish to English; we are speaking Irish, but using English words.

Language is the essence of culture. As the **seanfhocal** famously attributed to Irish revolutionary Pádraig Pearse goes: **Tír gan teanga, tír gan anam** – a country without a language is a country without a soul. In the latest Census (2022) only about 2.8% of the population of Ireland said they speak Irish daily outside the education system. However, Irish exists in a form when we speak English in Ireland, and all of the following phrases derive from Irish:

- He is, so he is.
- She's only after falling asleep on me!
- Sure, it's only yourself with the messages. Put them in the press!
- I would have known him at school.
- You wouldn't have another cup of tea, would you?
- Sure your one is after giving out to me for being bold!
- He's gas craic altogether.
- Says she to me …
- It's failed on me.
- You're as good. Thanks a million.
- Are you coddin' me?
- I've a fierce hunger on me.
- Any story?
- Would you cop on, ye little Jackeen!
- Smashing!

Certain expressions can sound 'foreign' to us, even though we speak English in Ireland. Words like 'shall', 'cupboard' and 'running errands' are commonly used by English speakers, but not Hiberno-English speakers. Instead, it's more typical to hear, 'doing the messages' in Ireland, referring to 'picking up some bits' or 'getting the groceries'. The word **teachtaireachtaí** – messages, comes from Old

Irish *techtairecht* ('message, errand, mission'). And the verbal noun of the verb **Tar** – to come is **'teacht'** so it's like a thing that is coming, e.g. **Tá mé ag teacht** – I am coming. **Tá na teachtaireachtaí ag teacht** – The messages are coming.

It makes sense that a message is a 'coming thing'. It's got an essence of movement, forward action and progress. Let's not forget the most famous Irish phrase with this verb, in its future tense, the slogan of Irish Republicanism: **Tiocfaidh ár lá!** Our day will come!

Older generations would treat the messages as an opportunity to collect the local gossip. Another great word, its custom sadly fading due to technology, is **bothántaíocht** – going door to door collecting the news, or stopping by for music, dancing and stories.

Irish has had a significant impact on the evolution of English words, some of my favourites being:

- **Uisce beatha** – 'whiskey' comes from the gushing, cascading onomatopoeic word **'uisce'**, meaning water. **Beatha** of life. Whiskey is the water of life.
- **Snas** – polish – snazz
- **Bean sídhe** – banshee (fairy woman, woman of the fairy mound)

- **Ag caoineadh** – keening (crying/wailing, especially connected to grief at the loss of a loved one)
- **Clog** – clock (The English word 'clock' comes from the Irish word **clog** meaning 'bell')
- **Smidiríní** – smithereens (**smiodar** – a broken piece or fragment)
- **Pus** – puss (having a puss on you, a sour face)
- **Slua** – slew (a crowd of people)
- **Bróg** – a shoe, gives us 'brogue'.

Along with these, some other words and phrases from Hiberno-English have seeped into the global lexicon of English:

- To put it on the long finger – **cuir ar an méar fhada**. Apparently, this is an Irish expression meaning 'to postpone indefinitely', and it possibly comes from the custom of wearing a ring on the index finger of your left hand if you are not engaged or married, on the second (middle, or longest) finger if you are engaged, on the third (ring) finger if married, and on the little finger if entirely disinclined.
- Making strange – this references the situation where a baby gets upset when it is placed in the arms of someone other than its parents. Apparently, it's unique to Hiberno-English, loaned from Irish,

where **coimhthíos a dhéanamh le duine** literally means 'to make strangeness with someone', or to be shy or aloof in their presence; **coimhthíos** means strangeness, shyness, aloofness or alienation. This phrase is said to come from the superstition that fairy folk were so jealous of human children they would steal a 'too-fair human baby' and replace it with a changeling. In Old Ireland, like in many poor societies, there was a very high mortality rate for women and children and a high rate of stillbirths and miscarriages. It was a way of understanding the inexplicable or the deeply painful, to think that the child a family lost was really a changeling, not a human child at all.

- 'Slogan' comes from **sluaghairm** – a battle cry! Brands are crying out to us with their slogans.
- In Ireland, we don't 'tell off' children when they're naughty. We give out to kids for being bold. 'Bold' means naughty, but it's a softer mischievousness which holds no malice. Giving out (telling off) comes from **ag tabhairt amach** – giving out. Calling someone bold, in Ireland, includes a hint of endearment, and is more of a mild disapproval rather than severe admonishment or scolding. It's a more affectionate way to recognise a child's

cheekiness, or boisterousness, and is often followed with 'you divileen', **diabhailín** – little devil. Giving out means something closer to 'complaining' rather than berating, chastising or criticising. In British English, 'bold' is confident or courageous, and 'naughty' is badly behaved, rude, disobedient. But in Ireland, it's nearly good to be bold!

- **Tá sí ag siúl amach leis** – She's walking out with him. This means to be dating someone, or seeing someone.
- 'Your man' and 'your one' come from **mo dhuine** – literally 'my person', to allude to someone when we both know who I'm talking about. This can be hugely confusing for people who insist, 'He's not *my* man!'
- In the English fairytale, 'Jack and the Beanstalk', we hear the rhyme – 'Fee–fi–fo–fum, I smell the blood of an Englishman. Be he alive, or be he dead, I'll grind his bones to make my bread!' Even when this poem first appeared in a pamphlet in 1596, Thomas Nash, the writer, said it was already old and its origins obscure. Charles Mackay proposes, in *The Gaelic Etymology of the Languages of Western Europe*, that the seemingly incoherent rhyme 'fee–fi–fo–fum' makes sense in Ancient Gaelic.

Apparently, the quatrain covertly expresses the Celts' cultural detestation for the invading Saxons and Angles.

- ○ Mackay observes that 'Faich' – meaning, 'behold / see' is similar to Modern Irish **'Feic'** (to see). *Fe* comes from **Fiadh**, meaning 'food', which means 'wild/deer' nowadays (and also the top girl's name in Ireland in 2021). *Fi* is from **fiú** (good to eat). *Fiú* means 'worth'. *Fo* means 'sufficient'. *Fum*, from Old Irish *feidhm*, meaning 'effort' or 'hunger'.
- ○ 'Behold, food, good to eat, sufficient for my hunger'. Notice the verb-first structure in the second part also – <u>Be</u> he alive or <u>be</u> he dead. This is in keeping with our structure of Irish.
- 'Slugging a drink' comes from the Old Irish *slog* ('to swallow'), from Old Irish *sluicid*, and from Proto-Celtic **slunketi*.
- 'Gobble' comes from the Irish word **gob** – mouth, beak, or snout.
- 'Phoney', meaning 'fake' comes from the Irish word **fáinne** – ring. Gilt brass rings used by swindlers were often falsely sold as real gold.
- Bog – One sixth of the island of Ireland is bogland.

Ireland contains more bog, relatively speaking, than any country in Europe except Finland. The word **bog** in Irish means 'soft', from Proto-Celtic **buggos* ('soft, tender'), perfectly describing this soft wetland that accumulates peat as a deposit of dead plant materials. **Bog** is also the verb 'to move' in Irish, pronounced /bug/.

- 'Crock of gold' – If you follow the most famous of the fairy folk, the **leipreachán** – leprechaun (coming from **lúchorpán** – little body), they might lead you to the end of the **bogha báistí** (rainbow) and there there will be a crock of gold. The word 'crock' comes from the Irish word for 'hill' (**cnoc**) pronounced /cruk/. In the west of Ireland, 'cn' can sound like /kr/, 'mn' as /mr/.

- 'As happy as a king' is how we say 'as happy as Larry' in Irish. And it goes like this: **chomh sásta le rí. Le rí** – with (as) a king, and **le rí** sounds like Larry. Apparently, 'as happy as Larry' comes from Irish! Other weaker theories suggest it comes from Larry Foley, a famous Australian-Irish boxer who never lost a fight and won a huge cash prize in the 1870s. Hints like this hidden in different slang words and expressions around the world remind us how the Irish travelled far and wide and brought the music and playfulness of language with them.

- Another one is 'I'll be there in a jiffy', which sounds similar to **deifir** – a rush or a hurry. This one has no solid linguistic evidence, but it might be a useful way to use sound association to remember it! **Déan deifir** – Make haste! (Hurry up!)

- Once, while I was planning an Easter egg hunt, I was struck by the word **tóraíocht** – hunt. This is where the word Tory derives from, and the Tories – the Conservative party in the UK today. The word **tóraí** means pursuer, or outlaw, or hunter! In the 17th century, after the Cromwellian conquest of Ireland, many dispossessed Irish people became guerrilla fighters or outlaws. These Irish rebels, known as '**tóraí**' (plural: '**tóraithe**'), fought against English rule, raiding English settlers' lands. The word **tóraí** originally means 'one who chases' but became associated with bandits or rebels. In the late 1600s, during political debates in England, the term 'Tory' was used as an insult for those who supported the monarchy (King James II) and opposed the Whigs. The Whigs called their rivals Tories to suggest they were like Irish Catholic bandits: dangerous and untrustworthy! Over time, the term lost its negative meaning (or did it?) and became the official name of the Tory Party, which evolved into today's Conservative Party in the UK.

- But guess what? The Whigs also get their name from Irish! The term Whig began as a short form of *whiggamore*, a term used for Gaelic-speaking Scottish cattle drivers who would call out '**Chuig**' or '**Chuig an bòthar**' – meaning 'away' or 'to the road', on their way to the corn markets in Leith. This sounded like 'whig' to the English corn sellers. Meant as an insult, the term was later used in 17th-century English political discourse to mock the Country Party, who opposed the succession of the Catholic James, Duke of York to the throne on King Charles II's death. Ironically, Country Party politicians adopted the label for themselves. So as the adage goes, 'what you resist, persists'. Despite a strategy to destroy the Irish language, it found its way into British political identity, and it stands the test of time.

All around us, in everyday life, we are living with Irish. You won't hear Irish people calling the **Taoiseach** the Prime Minister. He is our **Taoiseach** – our chief. The residence of our **Uachtarán** – President is **Áras an Uachtaráin**. You turn on the television and our national broadcaster is RTÉ – **Raidió Teilifís Éireann**. Although I really think it should be TG4, originally called TnaG – **Teilifís na Gaeilge**! Traditionally, to warm yourself up, you'd have turf or peat from **Bord na Móna. Móin** is turf/peat. Tuck into a **sneaicín** – small snack and you're looking at **Bord Bia** – The food board. Take a bus around and you'll be using **Bus Éireann**. Likewise, **Iarnród Éireann** – Irish Rail, or the **Luas** which means 'speed' and is the name given to Dublin's light rail system. To send a letter or parcel, we use our national postal service – **An Post. Bord Gáis** is the gas supply board. So, we're really living an immersive Irish experience.

When you open your eyes and ears to Irish, you'll start seeing and hearing it everywhere. Even big brands like Cadbury are catching on. A nationwide survey commissioned by third-level college Gaelchultúr, in conjunction with Amárach Market Research, gathered responses from 1,000 people across all age brackets and from all walks of life. The results are undeniable: Irish is good for business. Participants were asked about their perception of businesses that use Irish in their advertising and marketing activities. An impressive 73% agreed that when a business uses Irish, they assume it is local or Irish-owned. A very healthy 26% of respondents (36% of those under 35) said that they would be willing to pay more for the products or services from such a company.

Irish not only pervades our education system with terms like **Deis** (opportunity) schools and **Fás** (growth) courses, it reaches our senses in the world of theatre: **An Taibhdhearc** (ghostly vision) in Galway; in charities like **Trócaire** (mercy), **Suas** (up), and **Doras** (door); in restaurants and cafés choosing names like **Aniar** (westerly), **Liath** (grey), **Éist** (listen), **Plámás** (flattery). Like in the poet Paul Durcan's description of travelling to County Mayo as a child, and leaving behind the alien, foreign city of Dublin, these names can be like magic passwords leading us into eternity, leaving behind the alien, foreign language of English.

If you were setting up a **bialann** – restaurant, or any **gnó** – business, and wanted to give it an Irish name, **cad a roghnófá?** What would you choose? I think I would open a cocktail bar, called **Manglam** – Cocktail. This word sounds like amalgamation, and means concoction, mix, mash-up. I love how we hear the /ɒ/ sound, as in the 'o' in Clock, or Flop, in /mong-glum/. We are not saying /maan glaam/, although we can remember it by envisaging a glamorous man sipping on a **manglam** in a trendy cocktail bar. In my vision for a bilingual Ireland, revellers would order **as Gaeilge**, and there would be **deochanna** – drinks like:

- The **Ruaille Buaille** The mayhem/bedlam/hubbub /melee/rowdyism – what lark! Very fun to say. Try it out: /ROO-il-yeh BOO-il-yeh/
- The **Fuilibiliú** /FWILL-eh-bil-YOO/ – the hype
- The **Rúscam Raindí** /ROO-skum ran-dee/ – the commotion

And the slogan would be: **Áit a bhfuil tranglam, déanaimis manglam** – Where disorder prevails, let us make cocktails!

CLEACHTADH – PRACTICE

Déan machnamh ar na ceisteanna seo – Reflect on these questions:

1. **Dá dtabharfá ainm ar mhadra as Gaeilge,** If you were to give a dog an Irish name, **cad a thabharfá air?** – What would you call them? **Prátaí?** – Potatoes? **Pitseámaí?** – Pyjamas? **Rógaire?** – Rogue?

2. **Dá mbeadh gnólacht nua á bhunú agat agus ainm Gaeilge le tabhairt air, cén t-ainm a roghnófá?** If you were to start a business with an Irish name, what would it be?

3. **Dá mbeadh leanbh agat, cén t-ainm a roghnófá?** If you had a baby, what name would you choose?

(18)

Ag Iarraidh an Rud Atá Agat
Wanting What You Have

....

The Irish language has no verb 'to have', so when we want to say 'I have a dog, I have a book', we use the preposition (**ag** – at):

- **Tá madra agam** – I have a dog (is dog at me)
- **Tá leabhar agam** – I have a book (is book at me)
- **Tá cóta ag Seán** – Seán has a coat (is coat at Seán)
- **Tá peann ag an múinteoir** – The teacher has a pen (is pen at the teacher)

A helpful way to remember this might be that feelings are *on* me ('o' for on, 'o' for **orm** – on me) and possessions or things we have are *at* me ('a' for at, 'a' for **agam**).

We even have skills, and languages: **Tá Gaeilge agam** – I have Irish, so you might hear Irish people say, 'He has great chat!' or 'I haven't a word of Irish'. Well, that's an Irish structure!

With no verb 'to have', do we own anything? Are we attached to anything? Even saying, 'That's mine', or 'That's my bike' we say, **Is liomsa é** – It's with me.

I once heard a funny story about a school kid asking, 'Daddy! When the teacher holds up a lunch box and says **Cé leis é?** – Who is it with? Why do we have to say, "It's lumps o' hay!" back?' (**Is liomsa é!** – It's with me!)

With no verb 'to have', we have many needs. We say:

- **Tá sé de dhíth orm** – It is lacking/needed on me
- **Tá mé ag iarraidh** – I am wanting/needing
- **Tá mé ag lorg** – I am searching for/craving
- **Tá mé ag cuardach** – I am searching/hunting for
- **Tá ____ ag teastáil uaim** – ____ is needed from me (I need)
- **Tá ____ uaim** – ____ is from me (I need)

Notice how **agam** – at me, ends with 'm', like **orm** – on me, and **liom** – with me. And **agat** – at you, **ort** – on you, and **leat** – with you, all end with 't'. Many languages do this.

The word for 'mother' in multiple languages starts with 'm': Maman, Mãe, madre, мама, máma, mamma, **mamaí**! In Thai (แม่), Mandarin (妈妈) and Swahili (mama) they also all start with an M sound.

Apparently when children are starting to make sounds, one of the first and easiest sounds they produce is 'Mama'. Traditionally, the woman nursing them lights up and they reproduce those sounds to trigger a reaction. The infant is rewarded and they continue to produce that sound and associate it with their mother.

Mé is I/me in Irish and **tú** is you. When we look at other languages, it is similar.

- French: *Moi, toi* – me and you
- Spanish: *Mi, ti* – my and your
- Portuguese: *Meu, teu* – my and your
- Italian: *Mio, tuo* – my and your

In Irish, all the prepositions connected to me end with 'm', and all the prepositions about you end with 't'.

- **Orm** – on me, **ort** – on you.
- **Agam** – at me, **agat** – at you.
- **Liom** – with me, **leat** – with you.

- **Dom** – for/to me, **duit** – for/to you.
- **Romham** – before me, **romhat** – before you.
- **Uaim** – from me, **uait** – from you.
- **Asam** – out of me, **asat** – out of you.
- **Ionam** – in me, **ionat** – in you.

Irish is intricately patterned. It positions us in a way that is so alive and aware, that the self is separate from its surroundings. Things are within us, on us, before us, behind us. We experience a new way of existing in the world around us. It invites a fresh dimension to our modern-day existence and outlook on life. If we perceive that element of **freagracht** – responsibility as the answering we are called to react to, we notice an interaction with and respect for our surroundings that is akin to a higher level of consciousness.

There is a distinct chasm between ownership and possession, and **an Ghaeilge** approaches both in a different way than other languages. What does this mean for our consumerist, capitalist society to know deeply and intrinsically that objects and materials are never truly ours; they are at us or with us. And there is a truth of impermanence – things are always changing.

When I was working with another Irish-language teacher,

he brought up how he teaches the concept of **cuid** to his students. This word **cuid** – share/portion, is employed to talk about the amount of something we have. It can be a tricky concept to understand as an English speaker. At first glance, it seems obsolete or clunky, or unnecessary. He said, the difference between **Nífidh mé m'éadaí** – I will wash my clothes, and **Nífidh mé mo chuid éadaí** – I will wash my portion of clothes, is that in the first instance, it sounds like I am about to take all my clothes out of the wardrobe and wash every last item. When **cuid** precedes the noun, it clarifies that a certain amount is in question, not all.

In a conversation with Dian Killian, PhD, she noted that Irish is radically different from other languages in how we use **'cuid'** when asking how much money or how many cars someone has. What is your share of it? This tells us from an Irish-language indigenous view of the world that no one is supposed to have all of everything. We underestimate how these sorts of things affect our thinking.

Speaking of how our vocabulary and word choice affects our thinking, we just need to look at the word **aire** – care. We see this in **tabhair aire** – take care. **Aire** is the word for Minister in Irish and has links with Sanskrit. The Sanskrit word *Arya* has been translated to mean 'freeman' or 'noble one'. Imagine if ministers were called 'carers' instead. How would that impact their approach towards or our expectations of the role?

You might have heard this cautionary aphorism before: be wary of your thoughts, for they become your words, and be wary of your words for they become your actions, be wary of your actions, for those become your destiny.

This temporariness of not having, but things being by our side momentarily might teach us to look after what we have, and to know that the journey of life is like a symphony – it doesn't stay on one note, but should be seen as more like an Irish weather forecast: anything can happen, and we must enjoy the sun on our face while it lasts!

In English, 'owning' something seems efficient and transactional whereas Irish, with no verb 'to have' or 'to own', is more relational, non-attached and shared.

With so much wanting in the Irish language and no having; it reminds me of the Keats poem 'Ode to a Grecian Urn' about the passing of time, desire, fulfilment, impermanence, and transience. The secret to happiness is wanting what you have.

CLEACHTADH – PRACTICE

Scríobh liosta siopadóireachta as Gaeilge – Write a shopping list in Irish.

Tá úlla uaim – I need apples
Cad eile? – What else?
bainne – milk
arán – bread
oráistí – oranges
tae – tea
caife – coffee
pasta – pasta
plúr – flour
siúcra – sugar
im – butter

ola olóige – olive oil
brioscaí – biscuits
criospaí – crisps
coirce – oats
gránach – cereal
glasraí – vegetables
torthaí – fruits
seampú – shampoo
gallúnach – soap
craicir – crackers
cáis – cheese

19

Gaeilge sa Chorp
Irish in the Body

I was listening to Blindboy Boatclub's podcast episode 'A Thorough Meditation on Sparkling Water' **agus chuir sé tart orm** – and it put a thirst on me – to drink sparkling water. It also sparked a thought that in Irish, sparkling water is **uisce súilíneach,** coming from **súil** – eye and **súilíní** – little eyes. So the bubbles, the sparkles, are little eyes. **Súil** comes from the Proto-Indo-European word for 'sun' *sóh₂wḷ. In Irish mythology, the sun was the eye of the sky. 'Still water' is **uisce gan súilíní** – water without little eyes. I highly recommend Blindboy's podcast, and this episode in particular is excellent. It's about how the Irish in New York revered sparkling water because it reminded them of home and the holy wells which had naturally occurring carbonated or effervescent water.

Súil also means hope, or anticipation. **Tá súil agam** – I have hope/I hope (literally: I have an eye … /I have sun!)

- **Tá súil agam go bhfuil tú go maith** – I hope that you are well
- **Tá súil agam go mbeidh lá iontach agat** – I hope that you will have a great day

Irish is a time machine, connecting us to a worldview which predates capitalism, colonialism and the concept of a nine-to-five job. The stories of the Tuatha Dé Danann, Fionn Mac Cumhaill and Cú Chulainn aren't just dusty legends, they're reflections of our pre-colonial psyche, where nature, magic and the spiritual were entwined with daily life.

But come here to me, **cogar! Cogar** is a whisper, or entreaty to the listener to switch on. We don't mean, physically approach me, rather, I'm about to say something. People also use **goitse**, or **gabh i leith** to mean 'come here til I tell ye'. As we pull in, we push away:

- Away with you! **Amach leat!**
- Out with you! **Imigh leat!**

So many of our phrases come from structures in Irish. Reading Blindboy Boatclub's *Topographia Hibernica*, there are some gorgeous examples of Hiberno-English, lines that exemplify this kind of awareness of the body, how things are on us, at us, in us.

'A worry came over him.' In Irish we might say **tháinig imní air** – worry came on him.

'He held Cáit close in his two arms.' This reminds me of how my grandmother used to speak. It's a very conscious and mindful understanding of the body. 'Put out your two hands there,' my Nana would say. The experience of speaking Irish and thinking in Irish is deeply connected to the world around us, and the body we inhabit.

In *Small Things Like These*, Claire Keegan employs Hiberno-English in her writing, 'I'd no call to say that to you' and ''Tis not one of ours'. She often illustrates the evocative and intimate language of the body to convey emotion: 'He lifted me up and my legs dangled.' 'In his chest, some hurt was blooming.'

There are everyday phrases that sound identifiably Irish.

- 'Sure, your heart would go out to him!'
- 'Flat, monotonous voice on him!'
- 'Have you cash on you?'

If you heard an Irish person say, 'she's after breaking the window on me', you wouldn't be worried that there was glass shattered all over them, you would think someone disgruntled them by maybe breaking their window. Or if you said, 'don't be falling asleep on me now', there is no risk the person is physically falling asleep on top of you. They would just be falling asleep while you're speaking. Nearly worse!

This use of 'on' in Irish is really unique:
- **Cuireann tú meangadh gáire orm** – You make me smile (You put a smile on me.)
- **Cuireann tú bród orm** – You make me proud (You put pride on me.)
- **Cuirfidh mé glaoch ar mo sheanmháthair** – I will call my grandmother (I will put a call on my grandmother.)
- **Thug mé cuairt ar mo chara** – I visited my friend (I gave a visit on my friend.)

The idea of the body and how it serves our life is found

in verbs like **uchtaigh** – to foster/adopt. **Ucht** is a breast, chest, or lap. To give some encouragement or bolster someone with courage is to give **uchtach**. An adopted child is a **páiste uchtaithe**. I imagine a child you take to your chest, or take on your 'behalf', since we use **ucht** when thanking someone 'for' something. **Go raibh maith agat as ucht do chabhrach** –Thank you for your help. It is followed by the genitive, because it means 'for the sake *of*' – another expression comes to mind: **as ucht Dé!** – for God's sake!

The word **glúin** means both 'generation' and 'knee' in Irish. **Bean ghlúine** – midwife means 'woman of generation/a woman on her knees', or 'at the knees of the woman giving birth'. Women used to give birth on the floor, and to this day, many women report that the body craves that grounding and seek to be near the earth during labour. There is a growing shift towards more physiological or 'floor-based' birthing positions, like squatting, kneeling or all-fours, as they are seen as medically necessary to reduce pain in some cases. A midwife in ancient times was a woman who stood by the woman from cradle to grave, working for generations of women. We pass on these skills and stories **ó ghlúin go glúin** – literally 'from knee to knee', imagining a child sitting on a parent's or grandparent's knee.

We also have **bean chabhrach** – a helpful woman, and **cnáimhseach** – a midwife. **Cnámh** means bone, and **seach** comes from **seachas** – to avoid or offset. **Cnáimhseach** refers to the person who needs to know about the soft bones of the baby's head so they can pass through the mother's pelvis, being at the right angle so the baby's shoulders don't get stuck. To deliver a baby, in Irish, to bring a being into life is **éascaigh** – to ease. To ease, instead of 'to labour' – what a difference that shift would make to your mindset!

We hold a baby in our **baclainn** – in the bend or crook of our arm. There is no direct translation in English for this part of the body.

The amount you can carry under your arm is an **asclán** – very apt if you tend to go to the shops with no shopping bag, but refuse to buy one so you end up leaving with an armpit-full and something smushed under your chin, behind your knee, and so on. This armful resonates with the English word 'oxters'. 'Up to one's oxters' means up to their armpits. 'Oxters' comes from Old English *ōxn* ('armpit') cognate of Old Irish *oxal*, a cognate with Welsh *asgell*. **Ascaill** is armpit, in Irish, and also means 'avenue'!

The uilleann pipes are named for **uillinn** – elbow and they are played with the elbow rather than the breath, and this gives the name of the instrument a typically creative yet literal name. Uilleann piping is on the eminent UNESCO list of cultural heritage, including dry stone wall construction, hurling, harping and falconry.

Here are some basic words about the body:

> **Lámh(a)** – means both arm(s) and hand(s)!
> **Cos(a)** – means both leg(s) and foot (feet)!
> **Bolg** – belly. This is where we get one of our four Celtic festival names, **Imbolg** marking the beginning of spring. It means 'in the belly' because it's at this time of year that ewes have a lamb in their belly.
> **Droim** – back
> **Cliabh/ucht** – chest
> **Cíoch(a)** – breast(s)
> **Glúin(e)** – knee(s)
> **Uillinn** – elbow
> **Uillinneacha** – elbows (also used for 'angle(s)')
> **Cromá(i)n** – hip(s)
> **Gualainn** – shoulder
> **Guaillí** – shoulders
> **Rúitín(í)** – ankle(s)
> **Ceann** – head

Muineál – neck
Aghaidh – face
Súil(e) – eye(s)
Srón – nose
Cluas(a) – ear(s)
Béal – mouth
Fiacail – tooth
Fiacla – teeth
Giall – jaw
Leiceann – cheek
Leicne – cheeks
Craiceann – skin
Éadan – forehead
Gruaig – hair
Féasóg – beard
Mala(í) – eyebrow(s)
Croiméal – moustache
Cúlán – Medieval Irish mullet (coming from **cúl** back, and **lán** full)

Hair is on us, and eyes are at us:
- **Tá gruaig dhonn orm** – There is brown hair on me.
- **Tá súile gorma agam** – I have blue eyes.

Hair is a feminine noun, and typically so, with its slender ending. Since it is feminine, we lenite the adjective (we add a **séimhiú**, 'h', if applicable):

- **Gruaig dhonn** – brown hair
- **Gruaig dhubh** – black hair
- **Gruaig fhionn** – blond hair
- **Gruaig rua** – red hair

Súil – eye, is also feminine. **Súile** – eyes, are the plural, and they pluralise the adjective by adding an 'a' or 'e' depending on whether the adjective has a broad or slender ending.

- **Súile gorma** – blue eyes (**gorm** – blue)
- **Súile glasa** – green eyes (**glas** – green)
- **Súile liatha** – grey eyes (**liath** – grey)
- **Súile donna** – brown eyes (**donn** – brown)

There is a scene in the film An Cailín Ciúin (*The Quiet Girl*) depicting Seán, a middle-aged farmer and Cáit, who he is fostering for the summer, on the beach. Seán says, and it is translated:

> **Ní gá duit aon rud a rá** – You don't need to say anything
> **Cuimhnigh air sin i gcónaí** – Always remember that
> **Is iomaí duine nár thapaigh an deis a bhéal a choimeád dúnta** – Many's the person missed the

opportunity to say nothing
Is a chaill mórán dá bharr – And lost much because
of it.

A student of mine asked after watching the scene, do the
Irish hold silence in more than one way? The film is about
the unsaid, the unspeakable. Yes, this scene above reminds
me of the **seanfhocal** – proverb, **Is minic a bhris béal duine
a shrón** – It's often a person's mouth broke their nose. While
we have an aversion to speaking the truth too bluntly, we are
also wary of speaking too much, and as a people who appear
to fill every breath with speech, we also acknowledge and
respect the sanctity of silence. Another **seanfhocal** reminds
us: **Is binn béal ina thost** – It is a sweet mouth that is silent.

A **seanfhocal** is literally an old (**sean**) word (**focal**) – a
proverb. While many may have existed in oral tradition long
before writing, the earliest known examples appear in texts
like *Audacht Morainn* and *Tecosca Cormaic*, written down
in the 8th–9th centuries. They preserve cultural knowledge
and reflect moral guidance – the original life-hacks and
philosophies. Some of my favourites include: **Is fánach an
áit a bhfaighfeá gliomach** – It is rare the place you find a
lobster (Small world!); **Faigheann cos ar siúl rud nach
bhfaigheann cos ina cónaí** – A walking foot finds things a

stationary foot doesn't; and **Doras feasa fiafraí** – The door to wisdom is asking questions.

CLEACHTADH – PRACTICE

Amhrán – Song. Here is a little **éistphéist** – ear worm – to get you moving and committing these words to memory. The **is** here is an abbreviation of **agus** – and.

> **Ceann, gualainn, glúin is cos**
> Head, shoulder, knee and foot
> **Glúin is cos**
> Knee and foot
> **Ceann, gualainn, glúin is cos**
> Head, shoulder, knee and foot
> **Glúin is cos**
> Knee and foot
>
> **Agus súile, cluasa, béal agus srón**
> And eyes, ears, mouth and nose
>
> **Ceann, gualainn, glúin is cos**
> Head, shoulder, knee and foot
> **Glúin is cos**
> Knee and foot

20

Bíodh Eolas Agat ar na Focail agus is Leatsa Iad
Know the Words and They Are Yours

Years ago, I was shown around a house in Seville by my distant uncle, a language teacher himself, and he named each item in Spanish as we passed: *la manija de la puerta* – the door handle, *el fregadero* – the sink, *el armario* – the wardrobe. He said to me that when you know the names of things, they are yours. I've since learned that in Scottish mythology, knowing something's true name gives you power over it, and that in Irish folklore there are water-names and land-names and to call something by its wrong name is to bring bad luck.

Logainmneacha – Placenames

In a systematic and deliberate attempt to erase Irish culture, traditions, language, sport, dance, song and identity, names of Irish places were changed to anglicised forms – not based on their meanings, which were often deeply significant, but simply on how they sounded to the British soldiers who spoke no Irish. Brian Friel's play, *Translations*, explores this very theme. When you reflect on this incredible true story, in which the British anglicised the names of Irish towns and villages, the importance of **logainmneacha** – placenames – really hits home. **Logainm.ie** is a wonderful resource to find out how names changed over time. **Log** – place, **ainm** – name.

There are over 5,180 townlands in Ireland starting with *Bally*. This comes from **baile** – town/home and sometimes **béal** – mouth, if it's on the mouth of a river. Examples include **Baile Átha Cliath** – Town of the Hurdled Ford (the modern name for Dublin comes from **Dubh Linn** – Black Pool), and **Béal Feirste** – Belfast, Mouth of the Farset River.

We also have these common words popping up:
- Ard: from **ard** – high/height
- Beg: from **beag** – small
- Ben: from **binn/beann** – peak
- Bun: from **bun** – bottom/foot of
- Cill/Kill: from **coill** – wood, or **cill** – church/little cell
- Clogh: from **cloch** – stone
- Knock: from **cnoc** – hill
- More: from **mór** – big

- Shan: from **sean** – old
- Tra/try: from **trá** – beach

Sometimes people dismiss Irish as gobbledygook, but when you encounter a place like Glenageary, which means nothing in its anglicised form, I urge you to look at its original name: **Gleann na gCaorach** – Glen of the Sheep. It tells you its geographical features, its inhabitants. Knowing gives us power. Irish placenames are not nonsense – they hold nuance, memory and meaning.

When our sensibilities are sharpened, we can look at a signpost, at the Irish font that greets us and seduces us at every turn, and understand that Roundstone, County Galway in Irish is **Cloch na Rón**, meaning 'Seals' Rock', and nothing to do with a round stone. Ireland sometimes gets a reputation for quirky names, when in reality, none of these are as silly in their original form!

Some of my favourite place names include:

Termonfeckin, County Louth

From **Tearmann Feichín**, meaning 'Fechin's Church Land'. **Tearmann** in modern Irish means retreat, refuge or sanctuary.

Nobber, County Meath

From **An Obair,** which means 'The Work' referring to the Norman motte at the north end of the village.

Skeheenarinky, County Tipperary

From **Sceichín na Rince,** meaning 'The Dancing Bush'. According to a charming account written in 1911 and archived by **www.dúchas.ie**, a schoolchild collecting local lore recounted that:

> 'There is a lough, and according to the people 'tis from that lough that Skeheenarinky got its name. It is said that in the middle of the lough there grew a green patch, and on that patch there grew a Sgeach, the surface underneath the Sgeach was not firm, so that the water underneath used to make it bob up and down. And it is from that dancing bush in the lough that Skeheenarinky got its name.'

Glassillaunvealnacurra, County Galway

This comes from **Glas Oileán Bhéal na Cora.** This Galway townland, surprisingly close to its anglicised pronunciation, translates as 'Little Green Island of the Mouth of the Weir'.

Muckanaghederdauhaulia, County Galway

Muiceanach idir Dhá Sháile – 'Ridge Shaped Like a Pig's Back between Two Expanses of Briny Water' or, more simply, 'pig-shaped hill between two seas'.

Spunkane, County Kerry

Sponcán a place abounding in the growth of colt's foot. **Sponc** – pizzazz!

Lousybush, County Kilkenny

Sceach na Míol. In this case it's an actual translation. **Míol** – a louse. Incidentally, a 'whale' is a **míol mór** – a (very!) big louse.

The bilingual signage around Ireland is a statement, sparking our connection to place, telling a story, and highlighting the choice we have – the luxury we have of unearthing the ancient place names of our land.

Ainmneacha Gaelacha – Irish Names

Maybe you were surprised, intrigued, or even astounded, to find my surname to be Guidera. It is, in fact, and contrary to popular belief, an Irish surname. Some people assume it's my married name, but it's actually my maiden name. Pronounced 'correctly' by other people about 1% of the time, my family pronounces it /gaid–reh/ like 'Guide', and then /ra/. There are only about 160 Guideras in Ireland. At school, teachers would pronounce it /giddera/, /gideera/, /gweedra/ and /gidayra/. It comes from Tipperary and some roots include Mag Fhuadaire, from the Irish '**fuadaire**' meaning 'rambler'. In Irish, we would use Mac Giodaire for males and Nic Giodaire for females. At school I was Máirín Nic Giodaire. Another interpretation is 'Mac Giolla Dheara', meaning 'son of the servant of God'. It could also possibly come from **giodar** – haste. Versions include: Guidera, Guider, Giderra, Guidrey, Guidara, Gydera. And at the end of the day, there is even the likelihood that the name comes from **Mac Guidhir** – Maguire.

Growing up, my instinct, fuelled by my vivid imagination, was to search for some exotic origin. A quick online search might tell you that it's a rare Sicilian name that originally comes from Albania. One claim that I came across was that it was possibly a nickname derived from Albanian *vidër* (definite form *vidra*) 'otter', which I loved because the **madra uisce** – otter or literally 'water dog', is one of my favourite animals. So began a quest. I went to Albania a couple of years ago to see if I could find any Guideras. No results!

Now and again people say they know a Guidera. Sometimes it's a family member of mine and sometimes it isn't. It has been a source of pride, of course, but since there aren't many Guideras, I felt the need for privacy. I also felt a dissonance about being an Irish teacher, and not having an Irish sounding name. Even Mollie is anglicised. It would be Mailí in Irish. This feeling, teetering on a self-consciousness, linked with what other people think, is common with many groups and their relationship with the language.

Our association with our names is embedded in our psyche, a thread tying us to our ancestry and identity. To mangle the name into oblivion is to undo the layers of information, to deconstruct the meaning of it. To know you are a Sullivan, but not why, is a travesty. The surname Sullivan comes from **súil amháin** – one eye. Campbell comes from **cam béil** – crooked mouth. McNamara comes from **mac** (son) **na** (of the) **mara** (sea). Murphy, the most common Irish surname in Ireland and spread across the diaspora, comes from '**Murchadh**', which means sea-warrior or sea-battler (**muir** – sea, and **cath** – battle).

It both amuses and saddens me to see people with names like Kelly, Dwayne and Duffy writing comments online like 'dead language. Better off learning Arabic!' Friend, do you not know that there is no letter K or Y or Q in your ancestral language? Your very name is anglicised. Do not be defeatist. To know your name is to reclaim a part of who you are.

The Irish alphabet has no letter J, K, Q, V, W, X, Y or Z. The vast majority of Irish names – somewhere in the region of 99% – are anglicised. We think of Shawn, Shane, Johnny, Jimmy, Kitty, Kate, Molly, Paddy, Vinny, Quinn, Keith, Joe and Willy as being quintessentially Irish. They're all mutated into English spelling, and thus, become more English-sounding names.

There is still an aversion to Irish sounds, spellings, names and surnames. It might turn people off to see an Irish word because they fear not understanding it, or because they weren't taught it in a space that felt safe and supportive. This discomfort with the language can lead people to dismiss it. When people reject or denigrate their own heritage, we are reminded of the struggle Ireland has gone through and continues to emerge from. Throughout the centuries of oppression there has been a conflict between fighting for survival and maintaining autonomy, independence and, on a fundamental level, basic freedom and human rights.

One such example is the term **súpar** – a person who 'took the soup'. During **an Gorta Mór** – the Great Famine, the genocide of our nation, Catholics were starved to death. In order to stay alive, some people accepted a bowl of soup in exchange for converting to Protestantism. The act is still vilified to this day, seen by many as a betrayal of faith and identity. Some of those who took the soup dropped the 'O' in their name, distancing themselves from their Irish Catholic roots.

Irish surnames often include Ó or Mac. **Ó** means 'from', so the Ó Donoghues are those 'descendant of Donnchadh', a personal name composed of the elements **donn** 'brown-haired [man]' and **cath** 'battle'. A female's surname replaces Ó with **Ní** (reduced from **Iníon Uí** – 'daughter of descendant of'). **Mac** means son, and **Nic** is the feminine version of **Mac**. **Nic** comes from **Iníon Mhic** (daughter of the son). If a woman marries a man, she might choose to take his surname. In this case, **Ó** is replaced with **Bean Uí** ('wife of the descendant') and **Mac** by **Bean Mhic** ('wife of the son'). In both cases **Bean** may be omitted, which results in **Uí** or **Mhic.**

Words as integral as the names that bind us to our bloodlines, or the placenames that root us to our land and location, are worth holding onto. They are worth celebrating.

CLEACHTADH – PRACTICE

For many learners, a turning point in their journey is starting to see the street signs in a new light and they begin to decode their true meanings. The word contains a story. Irish can make us more receptive to deeper realities. As our poet W.B. Yeats said, in *The Celtic Twilight*, 'We can make our minds so like still water that beings gather about us that they may see, it may be, their own images, and so live for a moment with a clearer, perhaps even with a fiercer life because of our quiet.'

Choose five places you know or want to visit in Ireland and research their original names.

21

Is Mise Mé Féin!
I Am, so I Am!

The use of tagging on the affirmative, or even the negative –
it's not only the positives, so it's not – is a feature of Hiberno-
English that echoes the Irish language.

It comes from a structure called the equational copula,
which equates two things. For example 'I am the teacher'
where I = the teacher. **Is mise an múinteoir.**

In Irish, if we are saying what a thing is (it's a dog, she's a
doctor, it's a cup of tea) we use the copula. We can classify:

- **Is madra é** – It's a dog.
- **Is dochtúir í** – She's a doctor.
- **Is cupán tae é** – It's a cup of tea.

Or we can equate X=Y, when saying something like, 'That is my dog', or 'The neighbour is the doctor', or 'He is my brother'.

- **Is é Seán é** – He is Seán.
- **Is í Máire í** – She is Máire.
- **Is é mo dhearthái é** – He is my brother.

Since we often repeat the pronoun **é/í** – he/she in Irish, we translate this into English as 'so he is', or 'so she is'. Whether it's to fill a silence, add emphasis, convince the listener or yourself, or simply to speak more, it is incredibly common in daily lexicon.

You might hear a parent chastise their child: 'You're a little divileen, so you are!' It's almost like the speaker is pre-empting that the listener will refute. We are known to talk over each other. I'm reminded of the traditional Irish song 'Colcannon', performed by Mary Black. It goes:

Oh you did, so you did
So did he and so did I

There is a cheek to it, the neck of ye, to insist on what you're saying. A confidence. A smirk to storytelling. The verb-first emphasis is again at play. We are focusing on the action of the sentence, and doubling down on the information: 'She ran like the wind, so she did'; 'He is gas craic, so he is'; 'I'm as vexed, so I am'.

This use of 'as' is as interesting. In Ireland, we say, 'You're as kind', 'You're as good'. English speakers from other dialects might ask, as kind as … ? What's the comparison? As good as … gold? To hear a sentence like this, without prior knowledge of Hiberno-English, you might think it's a comparative sentence – You're as quiet … as a mouse? However, we use 'as' as an intensifier on its own. This could be because 'as' in Irish is **chomh** and it means 'so' as well as 'as'.

- **Tá tú chomh cineálta sin** – You are so kind
- **Tá tú chomh cliste sin chomh maith** – You are so clever as well

In Ireland, we tend to say, 'You're getting as tall!', 'You're as clever!', 'You're as kind', 'He's as generous'. There is no connected analogy. We simply mean: You are very tall, very clever, very kind; he's very generous.

- **Chomh ciúin le luch** – As quiet as a mouse.

- **Tá sí chomh ciúin sin** – She is as quiet (She's very quiet).
- **Chomh mór le bus** – As big as a bus.
- **Tá tú chomh mór sin** – You're as big.
- **Chomh bog le him** – As soft as butter.
- **Chomh folláin le breac** – As healthy as a trout.
- **Tá tú chomh deas sin!** – You are so nice!

We see **comh** when 'co-' would be present in English:
- **Comhghleacaí** – co-adventurer (colleague)
- **Comhghairdeas** – co-rejoicing (congratulations)
- **Comhrá** – co-say (conversation)
- **Comhraic** – co-kerfuffle (combat)
- **Comhluadar** – co-activity (company)
- **Comhbhá** – co-kinship (compassion)
- **Comhábhar** – co-material (ingredient)

Irish makes a lot of sense, so it does. She's as consistent! **Tá sí chomh comhsheasmhach sin!** Here we get **seasmhach** – unwavering, resilient, enduring – from the verb **seas** – to stand.

- **Seasann an focal i mo bhéal** – The word stands in my mouth (I'm tongue-tied; it won't come to me).
- **Tá mé ag seasamh leat** – I am standing with you – to console or grieve with a person, to offer your condolences – **do chomhbhrón** – your co-sadness.

One of my catchphrases is 'Are you classifying or describing?' Getting our head around this nuance is the key to unlocking how the structure of Irish works. Here, we can also introduce 'equating'.

We describe with the Bí verb. We classify with the Copula. You can think of it as 'descri**bí**ng' with the verb '**bí**' and **c**lassifying with the **c**opula. Usually, we describe using adjectives with the 'bí' verb, and we classify using nouns with the copula. But as you can see below, we can attach an adjective to the noun in the copula.

Describing:
- **Tá mé go maith** – I am well.
- **Tá sí greannmhar** – She is funny.
- **Bhí an lá go hálainn** – The day was beautiful.

Classifying:
- **Is múinteoir é** – He is a teacher.
- **Is múinteoir maith é** – He is a good teacher.
- **Ba lá iontach é** – It was a great day.

Equating:
- **Is é mo chara é** – He is my friend.
- **Is í an dochtúir an t-údar** – The (female) doctor is the author.

- **Is iad na cailíní na damhsóirí** – The girls are the dancers.

CLEACHTADH – PRACTICE

Are these describing, classifying or equating?

1. **Tá siad ard.**
2. **Is scannán uafásach é.**
3. **Níl siad blasta.**
4. **Ba dhlíodóir í.**
5. **Is é an sagart an t-imreoir is fearr.**
6. **Is fear cantalach é.**
7. **Is í an t-amhránaí is áille í.**
8. **Níl sé gaofar.**
9. **Is oíche ghaofar í.**
10. **Níl tú mícheart.**

You'll find the **freagraí** – answers to this exercise at the end of the book.

22

Imithe Thar Fóir leis na Dea-bhéasa
Politeness Gone Mad

....

'I would have gone to school with her!' 'He'd be a cousin of yours.' 'She'd be fond of the drink, so she would.' We often use 'would' as a lighter way of stating the truth or to talk about the past. It's a gentle nostalgia of sorts. Some people hate it. My aunt would say, 'No, it's not that I *would have gone* to school with her. I *did* go to school with her'.

- She would have been the doctor here for many years.
- I would be an avid reader, myself.

We may use this structure to cast our minds back to a longed-for past. In Irish, the **aimsir ghnáthchaite** – habitual past – **Bhínn** – I used to be, is very close to the **modh coinníollach** – conditional **Bheinn** – I would be/I would have been. **Bhíodh sé** – he used to be. **Bheadh sé** –

he would be/would have been. Also in English, it's common to use 'would' to connote a nostalgic or distant memory: I used to cycle to school – I would cycle to school.

Used in the present, it serves to distance us again, from **an fhírinne** – the truth.

Are the Irish a truthful people? Aren't we? Answering a question with a question is commonplace. The truth resides on a different level in Ireland. We take great care to please others at the expense of truth.

There is the trope of the three refusals. If someone offers you a lift – **'Ar mhaith leat síob?'** or a slice of cake **'Ar mhaith leat slis den cháca milis?'**, you politely decline three times, and then you accept. We are taken aback by directness. We might complain about a meal, but when the waiter arrives at the table, we tell him it was delectable! We tip him to convince him that it was a lovely meal and well-enjoyed, despite our strained insistence.

These days, Ireland is a thriving and multicultural country with a growing **geilleagar** – economy and high levels of **inimirce** – immigration – and **eisimirce** – emigration, and we are reminded of some of these ways that we are as a people. We might notice that a family member has lost some weight and no one mentions it, but then an in-law from another country where they have a much more direct approach, will straight-out say to their face – 'Wow, you are much thinner. What happened?'

Ní bheadh cupán eile tae agat, an mbeadh? You wouldn't have another cup of tea, would you? Does the speaker expect the other to answer in the affirmative, or are they looking for a negative response?

Is it a politeness, acquiescence, subservience, which is so at home in the mouths of the colonised?

We adopt these techniques of hedging and tentativeness to be more cautious, to be more diplomatic, and to avoid strong opinions. We lighten what we're saying, by prefacing it with 'I'd say' or 'Sure', to add a vagueness we will never be challenged on. 'Sure' here, not really meaning 'certain'. Sure, wouldn't you be a good lad for the singing yourself? 'Sure' used as a filler, as a marker, not of 'I am sure' but more a pragmatic marker in sentence-initial or clause-initial position (occasionally in tag questions), offering reassurance and expressing intersubjectivity in discourse. It affirms shared knowledge. A bit like 'your man' when we all know who we are talking about, like the inhaled 'yes' used to bond, to confirm connection or allow intimacy. It is saying: we speak the same language.

'Sure' functions as a pragmatic marker in Hiberno-English, often appearing at the beginning of sentences to express shared knowledge or offer reassurance. 'Sure' often serves as an epistemic adverbial expressing certainty or high confidence in a statement.

- He's grand, sure.
- Sure, I wouldn't know!
- Sure, you know yourself.

The conspicuousness of 'sure', occurring at the beginning, middle or end of an utterance, serves to emphasise the obviousness of a statement.

These quirks show how the Irish language was preserved in an environment where it was not encouraged, allowed or even legal to speak. Sure, wasn't it well for us? We can now trace back these structures. This preservation is similar to lilting (diddle–dee–do), which is often linked to times when singing or music was restricted or considered inappropriate, especially under British colonial rule.

One of the most effective ways of learning and retaining Irish is to think in Hiberno-English.

- **Nílim ach tar éis mo dhuine a fheiceáil** – I'm only after seeing your man.
- **Nach bhfuil mé chomh dána sin, a deir tú!** – Amn't I as bold, says you!
- **Tá sé tar éis tabhairt amach dom** – He's after giving out to me.
- **An mbeadh tú go maith?** – Would you be well?
- **Ar ndóigh, féach, seo é** – Sure look, sure this is it.
- **Seo é** – This is it.
- **Sin é** – That's it.
- **Sin sin** – That's that. (A great way to finish a conversation or fill a lull in chat.)

We would ask, 'Do you want to sweep the floor, there?' instead of 'Sweep the floor!'. We might say, 'Ah I wouldn't say that', if someone presents us with exactly what we want to say. Because we wouldn't say exactly what we think or how we feel: we're far too reticent, too wary, too sensitive to upset someone. We put others' feelings above all else. We sacrifice truth for social cohesion.

- **Ar mhiste leat?** – Would you mind?
- **An ndéanfá gar dom?** – Would you do me a favour?
- **Ní dhéanfá gar dom, an ndéanfá?** – You wouldn't do me a favour, would you?

We soften words, commonly using 'shite', 'feck' and 'arse' instead of their cruder alternatives. We say, 'Sure throw the plates over there' instead of 'Give them to me' or 'Hand them to me'. Making something out to be a question of whether it *might* happen distances us from the consequences. Things sound more hypothetical. It becomes more polite, vague, indirect.

Irish people apparently use hedging – beating around the bush – twice as much as other countries, according to a study by Farr and O'Keeffe (2002) called '"Would" as a hedging device in an Irish context: An intra-varietal comparison of institutionalised spoken interaction'. It's very challenging to be direct in Ireland. The beauty is, it's very easy to be direct when speaking Irish.

23

Cúig Mhíle síos an Bóthar
Five Mile down the Road

....

Have you ever heard someone say, 'Sure it's only five mile down the road'? Or, 'That'll be three euro', 'Throw in four pound of flour'.

We use an unmarked plurality. We use the singular form of the noun instead of the plural form. This way of using the singular form with the number has seeped into our English lexicon so that it's now an everyday part of Hiberno-English speech.

In Irish, when counting things, we use the singular form. Instead of three cats, we say **trí chat** – three cat. **Ceithre mhadra** – four dog. **Cúig theach** – five house.

Ireland exists in a kind of measurement limbo, with some people still using a mix of metric and imperial units.

My parents would say 'ten yard down there' and I would have no idea if that's near or far away. They recall the days pre-Google maps when it was common to ask a person for directions in Ireland. I suppose it could nearly be described as an act of giving directions.

The first stage of giving directions is scepticism. In rural Ireland a lot of tracing goes on. 'Who would you be now?' Then there is warmth and a keen desire to help, but not without criticising previous choices. 'Which way did you come from? Well, (scoffing) you've come the wrong way entirely! You'll have to head out towards the coast, cross over the bridge, pass the post office, and you'll come to a barn. If you see the donkeys that means you've gone way too far ... '

The directions can be so convoluted, it is reminiscent of the **púca**, a mischievous and shape-shifting creature from Irish mythology who plays tricks on you and leads the unwitting traveller off their path.

Some of the best stories about the **púca** – a creature found in Celtic, English and Channel Islands folklore – are those involving the malevolent trickster transforming into a horse, a goat, a cat, a dog or a hare and messing with rural or marine communities, and their retaliatory attempts at tricking the **púca** at their own game. The **púca** seems to appear late at night when the rambler is on their own and trying in vain to get home.

Have you ever heard about the **fóidín mearaí**? It is a **púca**-like myth local to Mayo. **Fód** means sod of turf, while **-ín** is the diminutive. **Mearaí** means confusion or bewilderment. If someone accidently stepped on this sod of turf on their way home, they would **go tobann** – suddenly – lose all sense of direction and not know if they were coming or going. Whoever steps on the **fód** becomes completely disoriented. There are **piseoga** – superstitions about what to do if you meet your fate at the **fód.** One is to wait for the fairies to grow tired of the game, or wait for the Guinness to wear off. Alternatively, you can take off your coat, turn it inside out and put it back on. Sometimes a red painted stone on the wall will guide you out of the trance.

Directions are not so straightforward in Ireland, but here they are, put simply in Irish:

> **Téigh ar chlé** – Go left
> **Téigh ar dheis** – Go right
> **Téigh díreach ar aghaidh** – Go straight ahead
> **Cas timpeall** – Turn around

Lean ar aghaidh – Carry on
Tar ar ais – Come back
Tá sé in aice le – It is beside
Tá sé os comhair – It is in front of
Tá sé ar chúl – It is behind
Téigh suas an bóthar – Go up the road
Téigh síos an bóthar – Go down the road
Tá sé thuas ansin – It's up there
Tá sé thíos ansin – It's down there
Tá sé anseo – It is here

Fíorchraic ar fad – Fierce craic altogether

You can have a fierce time of it altogether practising direction-giving **as Gaeilge.** Isn't this structure in itself gas altogether!

The position of the modifier here, 'altogether', after the adjective or noun, is unique to Hiberno-English. We say, 'You are brilliant, altogether!' 'Isn't she great craic altogether?'

In other English dialects, 'altogether' is used before the adjective: 'The show was altogether wonderful'. In Irish, we use **ar fad** to mean 'absolutely, all, completely, full, whole', literally: at length, and it goes after the adjective or noun, so we are mirroring this in Hiberno-English.

- **Tá tú go hiontach ar fad!** –You are great altogether /You are absolutely great!
- **Tá do shaol ar fad romhat** –Your whole life is ahead of you.

As I write this on Christmas Day in Dublin, it's fierce mild altogether. Google is trying to correct my English here, underlining 'fierce mild' and offering me 'fierce and mild' as an alternative. The word 'fierce' is used as a modifier to intensify the adjective. One theory is that it comes from **fíor** (true) or 'truly'. Situations could be fierce windy, fierce mild, fierce craic – the list is endless.

In Irish we intensify a description by adding **fíor-** as a prefix, and a **séimhiú** if the consonant takes one:

- **Fíor-álainn** – truly beautiful
- **Fíor-olc** – truly bad
- **Fíor-ábalta** – truly able
- **Fíor-aclaí** – truly athletic
- **Fíorshásta** – truly happy
- **Fíorthábhachtach** – truly important

We can also easily modify an adjective by using **an-** which means 'very':

- **an-mhaith** – very good
- **an-chantalach** – very grumpy
- **an-bhrónach** – very sad
- **an-ghruama** – very gloomy
- **an-fhlaithiúil** – very generous
- **an-éasca** – very easy

If the letters **DNTLS** come together, we know their sounds are produced in the same part of the mouth /duh/, /nuh/, /tuh/, /luh/, /suh/ so we don't add a **séimhiú** when they come together:

- **an-dána** – very bold
- **an-sásta** – very happy
- **an-te** – very hot

Seamus Heaney once said, 'if you have the words, there's always a chance that you will find the way'. The words have been guiding us. As a people, we are talkers. We like to spin a yarn, gather by the fireside and tell a story, put on the kettle and have an auld chinwag. A coffee and a yap. The words we use are eclectic. They're sharp, unwieldy and alliterative. We have an emphatic and hyperbolic turn of phrase. Instead of saying, 'It was a nice dinner', we want to say, 'It was absolutely delectable'. The more words and the higher the energy, the better. This may be due to the fact that our adjectives in Irish, many ending with the throaty and memorable '-(e)ach' /okk/, make such an impact on the story. They blast off at the end of the word and invite an expressive element to speech:

- **Salach** – dirty
- **Uafásach** – terrible
- **Brónach** – sad
- **Tuirseach** – tired
- **Glórach** – loud
- **Santach** – greedy
- **Marfach** – deadly
- **Cruthaitheach** – creative
- **Uaillmhianach** – ambitious
- **Fliuch** – rainy

Another common adjective ending is **-(i)úil:**
- **Dathúil** – pretty
- **Flaithiúil** – generous
- **Rathúil** – successful
- **Suimiúil** – interesting
- **Gairmiúil** – professional

And a third common ending is **-mhar:**

- **Greannmha**r – funny (**greann** – humour)
- **Grianmhar** – sunny (**grian** – sun)
- **Ceolmhar** – musical (**ceol** – music)
- **Luachmhar** – valuable (**luach** – value)
- **Ceomhar** – foggy (**ceo** – fog)

Sounds of words in English starting with 'd' can be quite depressing sometimes – disheartened, disappointed, despondent, dull. In fact, the letter 'd' is also very dramatically negative in Irish. The adjectives **dona** – bad, **daoirse** – enslavement, and **dorcha** – dark each have 's' counterparts, which are their positive antonyms: **sona** – happy, **saoirse** – freedom, and **sorcha** – light.

NOD IONTACH – TOP TIP

Descriptive words often have an air of drama about them **as Gaeilge**, much more so than their English translations. Try to include adjectives **as Gaeilge** in your everyday speech to add some dramatic flair to your vocabulary!

Some ideas could be **scriosta** – wrecked tired, or **préachta** – freezing cold.

CLEACHTADH – PRACTICE

Déan cur síos ort féin – Describe yourself

Tá mé – I am …
Níl mé – I am not …

Roghnaigh cúpla aidiacht – Choose a couple of adjectives.
To amplify the meaning, feel free to add **ar fad** – at length.

Tá mé blasta – I am delicious
Tá mé an-bhlasta – I am very delicious
Tá mé an-bhlasta ar fad – I am absolutely delicious

(24)

Níl Aon Rud Foirfe
Nothing Is Perfect

An bhfuil deoch ólta agat? Have you drink taken? This conjures up an image of an officious **Garda** with a thick midlands accent, questioning someone who's looking decidedly worse for wear. Have ye no homes to go to?

There is no Present Perfect in Irish. We don't have a structure akin to 'I have seen', 'I have done', 'I have eaten', nor do we have the Past Perfect (I had done) or Future Perfect (I will have done). Instead, we use **tar éis** – after. **Tá mé tar éis mo Mham a fheiceáil** – (literally) I am after seeing my Mum, I have just seen my Mum.

We're seeing a pattern emerge. We translate directly from Irish into English. This is how we kept the language alive, in our literature, our turns of phrase, our playfulness and flexibility with the language.

We could use the preposition '**ag**' (at) to depict having done something, for instance:

- **Tá an leabhar léite agam** – The book is read by me (I have read the book, or more Irish-sounding 'I have the book read!') or
- **Tá mé tar éis an leabhar a léamh** – I am after reading the book, which gives more of a feeling of recent completion, having 'just' read it.

'She's after making a hames of it!' To 'make a hames of something' is to mess something up or do something very badly. The 'hames' are a crucial part of a horse's harness, the metal or wooden bent pieces of the collar that help to distribute weight when pulling a cart or plough. If the hames weren't well made, it was a complete disaster for the rest of the whole shebang. (Interestingly, 'shebang' apparently comes from the French *char-à-banc*, a type of carriage with benches used for transport.)

In these structures we either use the verbal adjective – it is done/eaten/seen by me, or the verbal noun – I am after doing/eating/seeing it.

To form the verbal adjective, we generally add -te/-ta/ -the/-tha to the short verbs (one syllable), e.g.:

- **Déan** – to do; **déanta** – done
- **Ith** – to eat; **ite** – eaten
- **Feic** – to see; **feicthe** – seen

These three examples above with **Déan, Ith** and **Feic** are a bit special because they're all irregular verbs, but worth learning because they're more commonly used. We also use this structure to say' 'I'm impressed!' **Tá mé tógtha** – Literally, I am taken!

-ithe/-aithe is added to the long verbs (two syllables), after we chop off their -(a)igh endings, e.g.:

- **Tosaigh** – to start; **tosaithe** – started
- **Críochnaigh** – to finish; **críochnaithe** – finished
- **Dúisigh** – to wake up; **dúisithe** – woken up

We can use this verbal adjective to describe the state of something, too:

- **Tá an doras dúnta** – The door is closed.
- **Tá an fhuinneog oscailte** – The window is opened.
- **Tá an chistin glanta** – The kitchen is cleaned.

To form the verbal noun, for creating the gerund '-ing' form or 'to + infinitive form', we generally add -adh/-eadh/-eamh/-amh to short verbs:

- **Dún** – to close; **dúnadh** – closing/to close
- **Glan** – to clean; **glanadh** – cleaning/to clean
- **Seas** – to stand; **seasamh** – standing/to stand
- **Déan** – to do/make; **déanamh** – doing/making/to do/to make

And -iú/-ú to long verbs:

- **Tosaigh** – to start; **tosú** – starting/to start
- **Críochnaigh** – to finish; **críochnú** – finishing/to finish

Agus mé ag ithe mo dhinnéir! – **And me eating me dinner!**

You might hear this structure, 'and me doing something' in Hiberno-English, to mean 'while/when I was doing something'. This further illustrates the concept of presence and emphasis on the moment. The action is taking place and in addition to the action, there is a concurrent action happening: a person there, doing a thing, of equal importance.

- **Chuala mé cloigín an dorais ag bualadh agus mé**

ag ithe mo dhinnéir! – I heard the doorbell ringing, and me eating my dinner! There is an element of interruption here, of an unexpected incident.

- **Thosaigh sí ag caoineadh agus mé ag múineadh an ranga** – She started crying and me teaching the class.

This brings us back to a tangible awareness of all that is going on around us. There is a consciousness and aliveness to our environment, a call back to the present moment in Irish.

CLEACHTADH - PRACTICE

Which word is **ar iarraidh** – missing from the following sentences?

dinnćar/lcabhar/t-arán/lcaba/obair

1. **Tá an ... ite agam** – I have the ... eaten.
2. **Tá an ... léite agam** – I have the ... read.
3. **Tá an ... cóirithe agam** – I have the ... made-up.
4. **Tá an t- ... bácáilte agam** – I have the ... baked.
5. **Tá an ... déanta agam** – I have the ... done.

You'll find the **freagraí** – answers to this exercise at the end of the book.

25

Don Lá Atá Ann!
For the Day That's in It!

In Irish, when talking about what day it is, we say the day is 'in it'. **Ann** = in it/in him. It is the conjugated form of the preposition '**i**' – in.

- **Dé Luain atá ann** – Day of Monday is in it. (It's Monday.) From *Luna*, the Latin name for the Moon.
- **Dé Máirt atá ann** – Day of Tuesday is in it. From *Mars*, the Roman god of war.
- **Dé Céadaoin atá ann** – Day of Wednesday is in it. 'Day of the First Fast', combining '**céad**' (first) and '**aoine**' (fast), indicating the first fasting day of the week.
- **Déardaoin atá ann** – Day of Thursday is in it. **Déardaoin** means '**Dé idir dhá Aoine**' or 'Day Between the Two Fasts', referring to the period between Wednesday and Friday fasts.

- **Dé hAoine atá ann** – Day of Friday is in it. Meaning 'the day of the main fast'.
- **Dé Sathairn atá ann** – Day of Saturday is in it. Named after *Saturn*, the Roman god of agriculture, time, and liberation, similar to the naming conventions seen in other languages. **Satharn** comes from the Latin *Saturnus*, (e.g., Saturday in English, *Samedi* in French, *Sabato* in Italian).
- **Dé Domhnaigh atá ann** – Day of Sunday is in it. **Dé Domhnaigh** (Sunday in Irish) translates to 'Day of the Lord', derived from the Latin *dies Dominica*.

When we're talking about any time, period, month, season, or day, we use this structure.

- **An t-earrach atá ann** – The spring is in it/The spring is here!
- **An samhradh atá ann** – The summer is in it/The summer is here!
- **An fómhar atá ann** – The autumn is in it/The autumn is here!
- **An geimhreadh atá ann** – The winter is in it/The winter is here!
- **An Luan atá ann inniu** – It is Monday today.
- **Mo bhreithlá a bhí ann** – My birthday was in it/It was my birthday.

- **Lá iontach a bhí ann** – It was a great day.
- **An Nollaig a bheidh ann** – It will be Christmas.
- **Dé hAoine a bheidh ann** – It will be Friday.

We use this same preposition **'ann'** to say we can do something: **Tá mé in ann** – literally 'I am in in it', I am able.

- **Níl mé in ann** – I am not able. **An bhfuil tú in ann?** – Are you able?
- **Tá mé in ann** is synonymous with **Is féidir liom** – It's possible with me.
- **Ní féidir liom** – I can't.
- **An féidir leat?** – Can you?
- **Tá mé ábalta** – I am able.
- **Níl mé ábalta** – I am not able.
- **An bhfuil tú ábalta?** – Are you able?
- **Tig liom** – I can.
- **Ní thig liom** – I can't.
- **An dtig leat?** – Can you?

If we are telling someone they would make a good teacher, or artist, or they have something in them, we use this preposition, too.

- **Tá múinteoir ionat** – There is a teacher in you.
- **Tá spiorad iontach ionat** – There is a great spirit in

you (You are spirited).

- **Tá mo chroí istigh ionat** – My heart is inside you. A beautiful way to say 'I love you' in Irish.

Anseo Anois – Here Now

The Irish language in its expressiveness has a way of existing in the present moment. Learners can grapple with this meaning, and it's even been translated into Hiberno-English as nearly making everything 'now'. Someone might say 'Now' when they're about to put the kettle on, have just poured a cup of tea, about to stand up, just sat down, often accompanied with a clap of the hands. There are plenty of memes online that prove how common this is!

While the language centres us in the moment, the Hiberno-English use of 'now' is somewhat looser. We also tend to use 'now' when we don't actually mean *right now*. 'I'll get it for you now', 'I'll be with you now'. This is so commonplace in Ireland, we might not register it, but to other English-speakers, it's confusing and temporally inaccurate! Especially, the oxymoron: 'now in a minute', seems to sully the sanctity of 'now'.

The immediacy of **tá** (is/am/are) in contrast to the habitualness of **bíonn** (does be) brings us back to an indigenous way of thinking. Our ancestors had to be aware at all times of threats, of nature, of each other. Positioning the verb at the start of the sentence shows our emphasis on action, rather than agent. What happened is more important than who did it.

CLEACHTADH – PRACTICE

See if you can answer these questions. Sample answers given at the end of the book.

1. **Cén lá atá ann inniu?** What day is it today?
2. **Cén lá a bhí ann inné?** What day was it yesterday?
3. **Cén lá a bheidh ann amárach?** What day will it be tomorrow?
4. **Cén séasúr atá ann?** What season is it?
5. **Mo bhreithlá a bheidh ann Dé hAoine! An bhfuil tú in ann teacht?** It will be my birthday on Friday. Are you able to come?
6. **An féidir leat cáca a dhéanamh?** Can you make a cake?

You'll find the **freagraí** – answers to this exercise at the end of the book.

(26)

Teanga agus Smaointeoireacht
Language and Thought

Language influences cognition. Exposure to different languages shapes the way we think, and even has an impact on how we navigate our existence, how we talk about **grá** – love, **airgead** – money, and **bás** – death, and how we attribute **locht** – blame.

Agentive sentences in English, where the subject is achieving an outcome, follow a very basic format: the subject or doer of the verb (**an t-ainmní**), followed by the verb (**an briathar**), followed by the object (**an cuspóir**), which is the noun (**an t-ainmfhocal**) upon which the subject is performing the verb.

Mar shampla – for example, 'John broke the window'. John is the agent who performed the action. **Bhris John an fhuinneog.**

Conversely, non-agentive language lacks the agent. For example, 'The window broke', implies the window magically broke, and there was no agent present who actively broke it. The context in which it is used can have powerful implications on eye-witness accounts.

I was cycling home from a yoga class one day, and a thought came to me, as it often does in such moments of flow. I thought about ideas or statements I had never consciously said **os ard** – out loud, or even allowed myself to think. I thought, 'I can't have kids'. I'm not sure that I can, so it's not a fact. But it reminded me of **cumhacht na bhfocal** – the power of words. I immediately switched to Irish. How would I express that in Irish?

The idea that I can or can't have something that is out of my control seems bizarre. The concept that I have any agency is negated. We would sooner say, **Ní féidir liom páistí a bheith agam** – it's not possible with me kids to be at me, instead of me being the subject – the doer of any action. This way of speaking, in English, this linguistic structure has an impact. It adds extra pressure, reminding you that you can or can't do something, whereas in Irish it's not within your control. You don't own the responsibility of being able to do it or not. It is damaging to our spirit to think and speak in a language that discerns what we can or cannot do. Language affects our thoughts and actions. It shapes the way we see the world. It influences our choices and our conclusions.

I remember attending a lecture in university about performative language – legally or socially binding words: words that, once spoken, draw us into a contractual agreement of sorts. Like replying 'Yes' to **An bpósfaidh tú mé?** – Will you marry me? – can be potentially life changing. There are other phrases that carry weight too, like 'I promise' or 'You owe me'. Those words hold power, expectation, obligation. They shift the dynamic between listener and speaker, which makes them different to other interactions. It's from these examples that we can feel how certain words and ideas have a weight to them, and hold the depth of obligation or promise within them.

I had a conversation with Aoife Lowden, who is a **treoraí** – guide and **éascaitheoir** – facilitator of **cúrsaí** – courses, **searmanais** – ceremonies and **tionóil** – gatherings that aim to support in building relationships rooted in land-based ancestral **eagna** – wisdom. We reflected on the difference it would make for our chat to be in Irish rather than through English. We agreed it would be more dimensional, multilateral, and **machnamhach** – mindful, were it in Irish. Words like **dóchas** – hope came up, and we shared how the word in Irish means not an empty hope, as in, Oh I wish! But more of a steadfast knowing, a light which shines in the darkness and illuminates the way.

Seamus Heaney, **an file** – the poet, said: 'Hope is not optimism, which expects things to turn out well, but something rooted in the conviction that there is good worth working for.'

Words have the power to change not only the way we think, react, and feel, but how we live our lives. **Nuair a athraíonn tú an tslí a mbreathnaíonn tú ar rudaí, athraíonn na rudaí a mbreathnaíonn tú orthu** – When you change the way you look at things, the things you look at change.

27

Gaeilgeoir
Irish Speaker

Words have the power to block us and exclude us, but can also empower and propel us. In Ireland, some people see '**Gaeilgeoirí**' as a magical Irish-speaking elite. They're viewed as many things: gatekeepers of the language, protectors of the language, lucky, critical, wise, snobby, blessed, arrogant. The word connotes all these ideas, but the meaning is simple: a 'Gaeilgeoir' is a person who speaks Irish. It is fair to say that a huge number of people in Ireland, and around the world, want to speak Irish. But many people feel left out. I can hear the clear drop of their tone sometimes, or maybe it's a defensiveness, a fear – 'Ah, so you're a Gaeilgeoir then?' There are assumptions about Irish-speakers. But then there is a deeply held regret and longing to learn, to be fluent, to be connected. **A chara, is féidir leat** – My friend, you can do it.

Fluency is a myth. Well, our idea of it, anyway. Fluency doesn't happen overnight. It creeps up on you, when you least expect it, when you get an impromptu phone call and manage to understand the gist, or see an ad, or hear a joke, or have a dream and it dawns on you – I got that! I <u>twigged</u> that! I <u>dig</u> it! These last two come from the Irish verb **tuig** – to understand.

It happens when the stakes are high and you need to come up with a word or phrase on the spot, when you surprise yourself with your accuracy, when you invite challenge into your life and embrace it. When you learn to love the effort. **Tá sásamh san iarracht** – There is satisfaction or fulfilment in the effort.

Líofacht – fluency is a term for continuity, smoothness, pace and effort in speech production or language ability. None of these words mean **foirfeacht** – perfection. Learning Irish is about communication, confidence, community and consistency, unshackling ourselves from shame and decolonising our minds, connecting with heritage and identity, and experiencing a world within the words, a new perspective on reality, one which changes how we look at things, and how we live.

- **Ná bíodh eagla ort** – May there not be fear on you.
- **Tá ár lá anseo** – Our day is here.

It is your intent and interest to call yourself a Gaeilgeoir – someone who values the language, and who wants to speak it, who will take the opportunity to speak her. As this book is **ag druidim chun críche** – drawing to a close, your journey is beginning.

- **Tosaíonn gach turas le céim amháin** – Every journey starts with a step.
- **Tógaimis focal ar fhocal é** – Let's take it one word at a time.

It's an emotional journey, and it affects the diaspora differently to those who have been raised in Ireland and subjected to 'the way it's taught'. I regularly hold webinars online for up to 5,000 registered students. There are a few short **ceisteanna** – questions at the beginning and attendees tick boxes answering what motivates them to learn Irish. Is it **Clann** – Family; **Cairde** – Friends? **Turas go hÉirinn** – A trip to Ireland? **Eile** – Other? (**filíocht** – poetry; **damhsa** – dance; **litríocht** – literature; **spórt** – sport **san áireamh** included). Roughly 80% of the time they tick the box which says '**Oidhreacht agus Féiniúlacht** – Heritage and Identity'.

Students tell me they feel ashamed and regretful that they don't speak their native language. Others say they've been told not to speak Irish. Some say that Irish was impenetrable before my courses – they tried books, apps, teachers and other courses, and it never clicked. With patience, practice and persistence; with a method, motivation and mindset that works, it will click.

Lots of my students visit Ireland and use their Irish. They're told it's inspiring and uplifting. Some of them have moved to the Gaeltacht for a job! They give others an **ardú croí** – a lift of heart. Some new learners have no shame. They feel the joyous fulfilment of learning. **Ní ábhar í** – It's not a subject. **Is teanga í** – It's a language. They can't imagine people would see their own language as a burden. Coincidentally: **Eire** – burden; **Éire** – Ireland. The 'fada' makes all the difference!

How I see it is: If you love Irish, and you're learning, you're a **Gaeilgeoir**.

While my true ambition is to experience Ireland as a bilingual country, I understand that this aim is as similarly massive as a beginner saying, 'I want to be fluent!' and maybe not fully grasping what an intangible and slimy beast fluency can be. I tell my students, give yourself a smaller goal, like 'today I will learn numbers 1–10 in Irish', or, 'today I will learn the colours', or 'I will make some sentences with this one verb'. That way, you will be rewarded with success very often, and you will build your way to proficiency without having a huge and impossible goal with no gratifying steps along the way.

We must value these steps more than the ultimate outcome, because these little and big wins are what keep us going and what has an impact. Cradle the spark, add a little kindling, tend to the fire. It will continue to warm you and light your way if you encourage the flicker to grow. If a learner asks me how long until they achieve fluency, well that depends on effort, consistency, prior experience, aptitude, learning style and influences. I can provide a method, motivation, mindset, coaching, community, confidence and the craic. It won't happen overnight but it can definitely happen, and if you've reached this point in the book, you're well on your way. With even short bursts of engagement and focused effort, you can learn how to understand, enjoy and embrace Irish. Carve out some time for yourself to explore and enjoy this soul-enriching, life-affirming self-growth, and the results will amaze you.

Is leatsa í, is liomsa í – ár dteanga, ár rogha – It's yours, it's mine – our language, our choice.

Freagraí
Answers

Caibidil 2 – Chapter 2

Is fiú agus is féidir – It's worth it and you can do it

Grá mór – Big love (a great way to sign off a message or email)

Bain taitneamh as – Enjoy it

Bain triail as – Try it out

Ní thuigim – I don't understand

Tada gan iarracht – Nothing without effort

Caibidil 4 – Chapter 4

1. a
2. b
3. b
4. b
5. b
6. a
7. b
8. a

Caibidil 6 – Chapter 6

1. a
2. b
3. a
4. b
5. a
6. b
7. b
8. a

Caibidil 7 – Chapter 7

1. fíor – true.
2. bréagach – false. Agus tusa – And you?
3. fíor – true.
4. bréagach – false. Is mise – I am
5. fíor – true.
6. bréagach – false. I m'Éireannach – in my Irish
7. fíor – true.

Caibidil 8 – Chapter 8
Baininscneach – Feminine

an obair – the work
an oíche – the night
an tseachtain – the week
an mhúinteoireacht – the teaching

an ghrian – the sun
an ghealach – the moon
an chlann – the family
an Ghréigis – the Greek language
an lasóg – the little light
an tSeapáinis – the Japanese language
an Fhrainc – France

Firinscneach – Masculine

an sliabh – the mountain
an ceann – the head
an gúna – the dress
an páipéar – the paper
an lá – the day
an cat – the cat
an t-éan – the bird
an rud – the thing
an bricfeasta – the breakfast
an bia – the food
an t-innealtóir – the engineer

Caibidil 11 – Chapter 11

Someone announces their good news	**Comhghairdeas!** Congratulations!
Someone has a baby	**Fáilte chuig an domhan!** Welcome to the world!
Someone is looking great	**Tá tú go hálainn!** You are beautiful!
You want to support a sports team	**Corcaigh abú!** Up Cork! **Maigh Eo abú!** Up Mayo! **Éire abú!** Up Ireland!
Someone is nervous because they have an exam	**Ádh mór** Big luck
Someone is off on a trip	**Slán turais** Safe journey
Someone posts about losing a loved one	**Mo chomhbhrón** My condolences
Someone is making a delicious dish	**Tá cuma bhlasta air!** It looks delicious!
Someone is celebrating their birthday	**Lá Breithe Sona duit!** Happy Birthday!
Someone is celebrating with a toast	**Sláinte!** Cheers!

Caibidil 13 – Chapter 13

Dhún mé	I closed
Chuir mé	I put
Mhúin mé	I taught
Rith mé	I ran
Nigh mé	I washed
Shiúil mé	I walked
Cheap mé	I thought
Labhair mé	I said
D'éirigh mé	I got up
D'fhoghlaim mé	I learned
Mhínigh mé	I explained

Caibidil 14 – Chapter 14

grianghraf – photograph: **grian** – sun, **graf** – graph

spéirbhean – goddess, beautiful woman: **spéir** – sky, **bean** – woman

leathbhádóir – comrade, shipmate: **leath** – half, **bádóir** – boater

dea–scéal – good news: **dea** – positive, **scéal** – story

nuachtlitir – newsletter: **nuacht** – news, **litir** – letter

seanchara – old friend: **sean** – old, **cara** – friend

sráidbhaile – village: **sráid** – street, **baile** – town

seanathair – grandfather: **sean** – old, **athair** – father

gealgháireach – cheerful: **geal** – bright, **gáire** – laughter, **-ach** adjectival suffix

Notice how we add a **séimhiú** (underlined above) to ease the compound words together, unless DNTLS are in question.

Caibidil 16 – Chapter 16
1. **leadránach** – boring, **suimiúil** – interesting
2. **fliuch** – wet, **tirim** – dry
3. **ramhar** – fat, **tanaí** – thin
4. **suaimhneas** – peace, **imní** – anxiety
5. c
6. a
7. b
8. b
9. b

Caibidil 21 – Chapter 21
1. Describing – They are tall.
2. Classifying – It's a horrible film.
3. Describing – They are not tasty.
4. Classifying – She was a lawyer.
5. Equating – The priest is the best player.
6. Classifying – He is a grumpy man.
7. Equating – She is the most beautiful singer.

8. Describing – It is not windy.
9. Classifying – It is a windy night.
10. Describing – You're not wrong.

Caibidil 24 – Chapter 24

1. **dinnéar** – dinner
2. **leabhar** – book
3. **leaba** – bed
4. **t-arán** – bread
5. **obair** – work

Caibidil 25 – Chapter 25

1. **Dé Luain atá ann inniu/Inniu an Luan** – It is Monday today/Today is Monday.
2. **Dé Domhnaigh a bhí ann inné** – It was Sunday yesterday.
3. **Dé Máirt a bheidh ann amárach** – It will be Tuesday tomorrow.
4. **An samhradh atá ann** – It is the summer.
5. **Tá/Tá mé in ann teacht!** – Yes/I am able to come!
6. **Is féidir** – I can.

Nótaí Buíochais
Acknowledgements

Go raibh míle míle maith agaibh – Thanks a million, to everyone who brought this book to life. It's a **fíorú brionglóide dom** – dream come true for me. Ciara Considine, **m'fhoilsitheoir** – my publisher, **mo bhuíochas ó chroí** – my gratitude from the heart: **Is mór agam do thacaíocht** – I greatly appreciate your support, **agus do mhuinín** – and your confidence. **Mo mheas mór** – my big respect. Stephen Riordan, thank you for all the guidance and insights, to you and all the incredible team at Hachette Ireland: **Míle buíochas** – Many thanks! Claire Pelly, **is laoch thú** – you're a legend, **go raibh míle maith agat as d'obair iontach** – thank you for your wonderful work. Gráinne Ní Mhuilneoir, **táim faoi chomaoin mhór agat as d'obair, do chúram agus do shúil seabhaic** I am indebted to you for your work, your attentiveness, and your eagle eye!

Mo thuismitheoirí agus mo dheartháireacha – My parents and brothers, **tá mé an-bhuíoch** – I'm very grateful. Thank you for championing my penmanship and supporting my journeys. **Tá grá agam daoibh** – I love you.

Tá buíochas ar leith ag dul daoibh – Special thanks to you, Lucy Sweeney Byrne and George Syborn for the encouragement and excitement, always. **Go raibh maith agaibh** – Thank you Manuela and Zé Manel, and Anita and Don. **Is é an pobal an múinteoir é** – The community is the teacher.

Ba mhaith liom m'fhíorbhuíochas a chur in iúl duit – I would like to express my true thanks to you, Richard Spatafora, for sharing so much more than rants across the Atlantic: **eagna** – wisdom, **cairdeas** – friendship agus **cuid mhaith grinn** – and a good dose of humour. Thank you for being the best example of what's possible when we throw our heart and soul into something.

Lisa Friedman, my beloved writing teacher, who let me give up on my writing to go and explore Irish with Mollie, and welcomed me back as if knowing that this was what I was meant to write about the whole time. Deirdre Madden, thank you for teaching me that the writer needs talent and the talent needs work.

To the Basque Country, Spain, Portugal, Hungary, Japan and all the people I've met along the way who helped me feel at home around the world, and gave me a **léargas maith ar**

Éirinn ó i bhfad i gcéin – a good view of Ireland from afar.

Rith – running, **ióga** – yoga **agus damhsa** – and dancing … **Go raibh maith agaibh as ligean dom smaoineamh agus análú níos fearr** – Thank you for letting me think and breathe better.

To the people of Inis Mór: Niall Madigan, Olwen agus Mícheál Ó Goill, Deirdre Ní Chinnéide, Úna Mc Donagh, Fionnuala Hernon O'Flaherty, Noel Mahon, agus PJ Ó Flaitheartá. Thank you for bringing the essence of this book into the community for MollieFest 2025.

To the language teachers, influencers and creators, polyglots, and linguists from whom I've learned and who share their knowledge so beautifully. Manchán Magan, **Go raibh míle maith agat as do mheon oscailte** – Thank you for your open mind. Italki, thank you in all the languages you teach, for putting me on this path. Thanks to Nualeargais, Oideas Gael, Breandán Kenny, Daniel, my Celta teacher Alison Elliott, and my friend and teaching mentor Sarah Clow. Thank you, International House, and everyone I met there, for teaching me about teaching.

Davide and Elena, thank you for everything.

To my podcast guests who helped me ground these ideas and live these ideals in action. Thank you for sharing your passion and rethinking and revitalising Irishness with me. To everyone who has invited me to speak – thank you for giving Irish a voice and a chance.

To all my followers, listeners, readers, for all the likes and messages and comments and community we have built. For using what you're learning.

To my first students leading me to my forever students, far and wide, **grá mór** – big love. **Go raibh maith agaibh as bhur bhfuinneamh** – Thank you for your energy, **an chraic** – the craic, **na ceisteanna** – the questions, **an iarracht** – the effort **agus an chomhsheasmhacht** – and the consistency you devote to your lessons. **Spreagann sibh mé gach lá** – You inspire me every day.

Coláiste Chamuis, an Tulach, you kicked me out and it was one of the worst episodes of my young life, but I doubt I would have had this journey without your input. **Go raibh maith agat as gliondar na Gaeilge a thaispeáint dom** – Thank you for showing me the joy of Irish.

Mo shinsir – My ancestors. Nana, **grá mór.**

Mo nia – My nephew Robin, **agus mo neacht** – and my niece, Indie, **go labhraí sibh le bród** – May ye speak with pride.

Pedro, **mo leathbhádóir** – the one who rows the boat with me, thank you for your love, strength, patience, support, motivation and inspiration through all the waves.

Sign up for my courses here with a special reader's discount

www.irishwithmollie.com/onlineacademy-book

Special Reader Offer – Scan the QR code for your Special Reader Offer from Irish with Mollie!

'This is my fourth attempt learning Irish spread out over 40 years. Until I started your course, I could not get my arms around it. Irish remained impenetrable for me until your course.'

JOHN, USA

....

'It feels like a friend is helping me learn the language and I love that!'

LAURA, IRELAND

....

'This course is so well-laid out, so handy and easy to follow! Everything is clicking like you said it would!'

DEIRDRE, UK

....

'You have shed light on so many questions I had. This course is really engaging and interesting!'

PETER, CANADA

....

'Learning with you is the highlight of my day!'

BEATRICE, FRANCE

To Pedro,
mo sholas my light, **mo shuaimhneas** my peace

IRISH
With Mollie

THE

GAEILGE

GUIDE

Spark Your Connection to
the Irish Language and Legacy

HACHETTE
BOOKS
IRELAND

First published in Ireland in 2025 by
HACHETTE BOOKS IRELAND

2

Motifs of the flame and match: Shutterstock.com

Cataloguing in Publication Data is available from the British Library

ISBN 978 1 39975 158 2

Typeset in Minion Pro by Slick Fish Design

Printed and bound in Great Britain by
Clays Ltd, Elcograf S.p.A

Hachette Books Ireland policy is to use papers that are natural, renewable and
recyclable products and made from wood grown in sustainable forests. The logging
and manufacturing processes are expected to conform to the environmental
regulations of the country of origin.

Hachette Books Ireland
8 Castlecourt Centre
Castleknock
Dublin 15, Ireland
(email: info@hbgi.ie)

Authorised representative in the EEA

A division of Hachette UK Ltd
Carmelite House, 50 Victoria Embankment, London EC4Y 0DZ

www.hachettebooksireland.ie

THE GAEILGE GUIDE

GUIDE

Spark Your Connection to
the Irish Language and Legacy

Mollie Guidera is an educator, writer, and language activist, weaving storytelling and etymology into her innovative teaching methods, celebrating and nurturing identity and heritage connections. She studied at Trinity College, Dublin and earned her teaching qualification from the University of Cambridge. She brings depth, clarity, and creativity to language learning.

She offers accessible, relatable resources on her website www.irishwithmollie.com, on Instagram and TikTok @ irishwithmollie, in her newsletter, and through her podcast, 'Irish with Mollie'. Her creative workshops, retreats, and courses demystify the language and explore the healing and soulful path of effective learning.

Offline, Mollie enjoys running, reading, dancing, yoga, and swimming in the sea. *The Gaeilge Guide* is her first book.